THE WORLD'S WORST
SCANDALS
SEX, LIES AND CORRUPTION

TERRY BURROWS

ARCTURUS

PICTURE CREDITS

All pictures from Getty Images, except pages 84, 85, 86 and 87 (Library of Congress) and 57 (b), 93 (Shutterstock)

This edition published in 2019 by Arcturus Publishing Limited
26/27 Bickels Yard, 151–153 Bermondsey Street,
London SE1 3HA

Copyright © Arcturus Holdings Limited

ISBN: 978-1-78950-366-1
AD007180UK

Printed in China

CONTENTS

INTRODUCTION: WHY DO WE LOVE SCANDAL?

'The public have an insatiable curiosity to know everything except what is worth knowing ... The private lives of men and women should not be told to the public. The public have nothing to do with them at all.'

OSCAR WILDE, 1891

These words would soon have greater personal significance than Oscar Wilde ever could have imagined. Only four years later, the salacious minutiae of the celebrated playwright's relationship with Lord Alfred Douglas were bandied about all over the British press. Readers couldn't get enough. If we look at it dispassionately, all of the ingredients were in place for a perfect scandal.

It had the accusation. Douglas's estranged father, the Marquis of Queensberry, left a calling card at Wilde's club inscribed: 'For Oscar Wilde, posing sodomite.' (Homosexuality at this time was not only against the law but was viewed as the most shocking of personal transgressions.)

It had hubris. Even though Wilde knew the allegation to be essentially true, against the advice of friends he initiated a private libel prosecution against Queensberry, claiming the card was effectively a public accusation of the crime of sodomy.

Queensberry either had to admit the libel or prove its truth.

It had a sensational trial. Queensberry hired private detectives who quickly discovered plenty of evidence of Wilde's numerous liaisons. In scenes of near hysteria in the public gallery, the court heard accounts of Wilde's 'homosexual underworld' of brothels, male prostitutes and transvestites. On the advice of his lawyer, since Queensberry's allegation was deemed 'true in substance and in fact', Wilde dropped the case, but he was nonetheless deemed liable for Queensberry's legal expenses. And that bankrupted him.

And it had a sensational coda. The moment Wilde left the courtroom a warrant was filed for his arrest on charges of sodomy and gross indecency and at a second shocking trial he was found guilty and sentenced to two years in prison. Released in May 1897, he fled Britain a broken man and died in France three years later.

A contemporary observer would regard the Oscar Wilde scandal as a thoroughly tragic business. With homosexuality legal since 1967 in the United Kingdom and Lord

Alfred Douglas a consenting adult, no law would have been broken in the present day. Looking back, the only scandal we see is that a man was jailed for 'the love that dare not speak its name'.

THUMBS-UP OR THUMBS-DOWN?

A cynic might say that many of the sex scandals that have appeared in the press since then have been published with the sole purpose of titillating the reader and bringing out the supposed voyeur in us all. In this way we suddenly find ourselves sucked into the narrative, caring about the people, their lives and the details of the unfolding story. Of course, we are bound to find some scandals shocking. We are perhaps drawn to these in a similar way to viewing a horror film. We can experience outrage, terror and empathy safe in the knowledge that none of this is happening to us.

A scandal can also provide a different kind of escapism, a temporary respite from our own problems. We take solace in the fact that the woes and complexities we may face in our own lives are manageable by comparison.

All scandals by their very nature involve the breaking of rules. If not the rule of law then the rules of social acceptability. And while at some time we are all surely tempted to push back those boundaries, we generally don't. We can, however, take vicarious pleasure in the transgressions of others: while we succeed in resisting temptation ourselves, we perhaps admire them for giving in to their desires. And we think to ourselves, 'Maybe ... one day ...'

Perhaps it's a fundamental component of the human condition that we also want to see justice served, taking simple joy in seeing the bad guy getting his comeuppance. We want there to be a consequence, be it shameful public humiliation, loss of career and material wealth or – in the most deserving cases – incarceration. We want good to triumph and evil to fail. Just like in the movies.

Ultimately, a scandal gives us the opportunity to exercise the power to forgive. The disgraced idol – whose prospects are now uncertain – knows that he's let us down and begs for absolution. His future is in our hands. Like a Roman crowd passing judgement on a defeated gladiator, our thumbs are poised. Up or down? Which is it to be?

SCANDALOUS THOUGHTS

This leads to the inevitable question: what actually constitutes a scandal? The roots of the word derive from the ancient Greek *skándalon*: literally 'a cause of moral stumbling'. Our modern understanding of it comes from its evolution through Old English (*scand*), Old High German (*scanda*) and Middle French (*scandale*), all of which extends the idea of moral failing or misconduct with a consequence: ignominy, disgrace or damage to a reputation. Unsurprisingly, the word's early uses were mainly theological – it principally described transgressive behaviour that brought about religious censure. Today the word has a broader spectrum of interpretations, but it is most commonly used when a person's standing in society is damaged through immoral or offensive conduct ... or malicious gossip, whether true or not. (It's no coincidence that scandal and slander both share the same etymological roots.)

ANCIENT SINS

Of course, a scandal only becomes a scandal if it's deemed to be so by others. And that can differ between communities and places and over time. Tales of debauchery among the elite of ancient Rome are legion, but while the murder, rape and incest that took place in the household of Caligula would have created a public outcry and censure had they happened in any royal family of the past few centuries, these were not scandals in the modern sense. Caligula was the emperor and it was accepted that he could do whatever he liked! (As it happens, accounts of the time by Seneca the Younger were hardly complimentary to Caligula – he is described as an insane, self-absorbed, sexually perverted murderer – but he eventually got his comeuppance at the hands of his own Praetorian Guard.)

> ... a person's standing in society is damaged through immoral or offensive conduct.

One of the earliest documented public scandals took place in ancient Egypt. The Judicial Papyrus of Turin tells in detail the story of the so-called 'harem conspiracy', a plot to murder pharaoh Ramesses III in 1155 BC. Egypt under the rule of the unpopular Ramesses was in domestic decline and one of the pharaoh's lesser wives, Queen Tiye, sought to overthrow her weak husband and replace him with her son, Pentewere. While the pharaoh was enjoying an evening with his royal harem in Thebes, an attempt was made on his life. The plotters included wives, officials and servants and his personal physician and court magician employed spells and incantations to make him more vulnerable.

Tiye's plot was only partially successful: Ramesses III was indeed murdered, with multiple assassins slitting his throat and removing parts of his body with an axe, but his son and chosen heir Ramesses IV quickly took up the reins of power. Sensing that the episode could result in public outrage and be an embarrassment for an already ailing royal family, the new pharaoh swiftly convened a trial of the conspirators. The papyrus provides fascinating detail of the charges against the 32 men and six women, along with their verdicts and sentences. Most were burned to death and their ashes scattered in public in the streets; others were compelled to commit suicide. There is no record of what happened to Queen Tiye, although we can imagine that her reputation within the royal household might have been somewhat tarnished.

READ ALL ABOUT IT!

The reason why the modern-day scandal is far more commonplace is down to the way communications have evolved. News of the harem conspiracy will have spread quickly through royal and court circles, but the ripple of information beyond will have been slow as it would mostly have been passed on by word of mouth. This changed with the invention of the printing press in the 15th century, which enabled news pamphlets and corantos – the precursor to the newspaper – to be published and disseminated. It wasn't until the start of the 18th century that eminent figures began to realize the ways in which the printed

Journalist and socialite Lady Colin Campbell was an early victim of the popular press.

word could have an impact on the way they were perceived by their public. America's first great political sex scandal – the Hamilton–Reynolds affair of 1791 (see Sex and the Founding Fathers) – only became public knowledge when a pamphleteer decided to publish the story. Even though a good deal of the pamphlet's content was untrue, it largely destroyed the presidential ambitions of Alexander Hamilton – at that time, after President George Washington himself, the most important figure within the US government.

The first true newspapers were sober and neutral in tone. In 1843, however, publisher John Browne Bell addressed what he saw as a gap in the market when he launched the *News of the World* in Britain. It was the cheapest newspaper of its time and it was aimed squarely at the newly literate working classes; by this time around three-quarters of the population of Europe and the United States were capable of reading. Bell rightly believed that a newspaper concentrating on crime, sensation, scandal and vice would be a hit with the readers. The first major scandal he covered was the case of Campbell versus Campbell, in which society figure Lady Colin Campbell was seen by her butler (looking through the keyhole, of course) engaging in 'steamy sex sessions'.

Crowds gathered outside the courtroom and her London home, and she was branded 'a common harlot' by the newspaper. By 1950, the *News of the World* was the biggest-selling newspaper in the world and had already provided a template for similar titles in most other countries.

The *News of the World* was also a pioneer of the practice of 'cheque book journalism'. Generally considered unethical in America, European tabloids have long been known to pay sources – often disreputable or criminal – for their information. In a sex scandal this may have meant, for example, that a prostitute could earn a fee by 'testifying' in print that her services had been hired by, say, a well-known politician (see A Twist in the Tale).

EARLY INVESTIGATIONS

In 1906, President Theodore Roosevelt coined the term 'muckraking' (which he derived from John Bunyan's *The Pilgrim's Progress*) in reference to reform-minded journalists of America's so-called 'progressive era'. This was the first generation of investigative or 'watchdog' journalism, where politicians, political parties or powerful corporations could find themselves under scrutiny from reporters with an agenda of social change or the documentation of wrongdoing. The first important journal of this type was *McClure's Magazine* of New York City, whose pioneering reporter Ida Tarbell produced a series of influential stories in 1902 that brought monopoly abuses within John D. Rockefeller's Standard Oil to the attention of the public. President Roosevelt, like many other powerful figures, saw these journalists as a nuisance who impeded their work, as did one of his successors, Richard Nixon, 70 years later. When the two most celebrated muckrakers of their time – *Washington Post* reporters

Bob Woodward and Carl Bernstein – revealed the 1972 Watergate scandal (see Watergate), their efforts showed that President Nixon had lied to the American people. Rather than face inevitable impeachment, he chose to resign.

THE SOCIAL MEDIA ERA

Just as radio and television came to revolutionize the world of communication in the 20th century, the Internet would similarly cast its shadow over the dawn of the 21st. And the most radical changes came with the global uptake of popular social media applications, like Twitter, Instagram, YouTube and, the king of them all, Facebook. By the start of 2019 there were 2.32 billion monthly active users of Facebook throughout the world and this began a radical overhaul of the way in which information was distributed. Indeed, more people now get their news from social media sites than from printed newspapers.

One of the most appealing aspects of social media is the sheer speed at which information can be shared. Twitter is particularly popular among public figures; since communiqués ('tweets') must be brief (a maximum of 280 characters long), they are ideal for broadcasting soundbites. A tweet can take a few seconds to write and transmit to the smartphones of many millions of followers. (Singer Katy Perry, the most popular person on Twitter, has well over a hundred million followers.)

Twitter is also the ideal format for making an ill-considered, career-defining post when someone is in an emotional state or under the influence of drink or drugs. Comedian Roseanne Barr discovered this the hard way. In the early hours of 29 May 2018, she responded to a tweet about former President Obama's aide Valerie Jarrett, an Iranian-born woman of mixed European and African American descent. She thought she was making an edgy political quip ('muslim brotherhood & planet of the apes had a baby=vj'), but it was widely interpreted as a horribly racist remark. Minutes later she found herself at the centre of a torrential Twitter storm and hours later ABC Entertainment had cancelled her TV show, *Roseanne*, describing her jibe as 'repugnant'. In her own defence, Barr claimed that the tweet had been made at 2 a.m. under the influence of the sedative Ambien, but Sanofi, the company that produces the drug, gave its own tart response on Twitter: 'Racism is not a known side effect of any Sanofi medication'.

A career as one of America's most successful comedy actresses was demolished in a matter of seconds.

Clearly we can't possibly discuss social media without a mention of President Donald J. Trump, a man who some would say has turned the controversial stream-of-consciousness tweet into an art form. His frequent remarks – he tweeted on more than 2,500 occasions during his first year in office – are capable of causing stock market fluctuations, frustrating White House staff, angering foreign governments and offending huge segments of the American public into the bargain.

We can only guess where this kind of technology is likely to lead us in the future. What is certain, though, is that, whatever form it might take, our appetite for good old-fashioned scandal is unlikely to be diminished. And perhaps that's something we just have to chalk up to basic human nature.

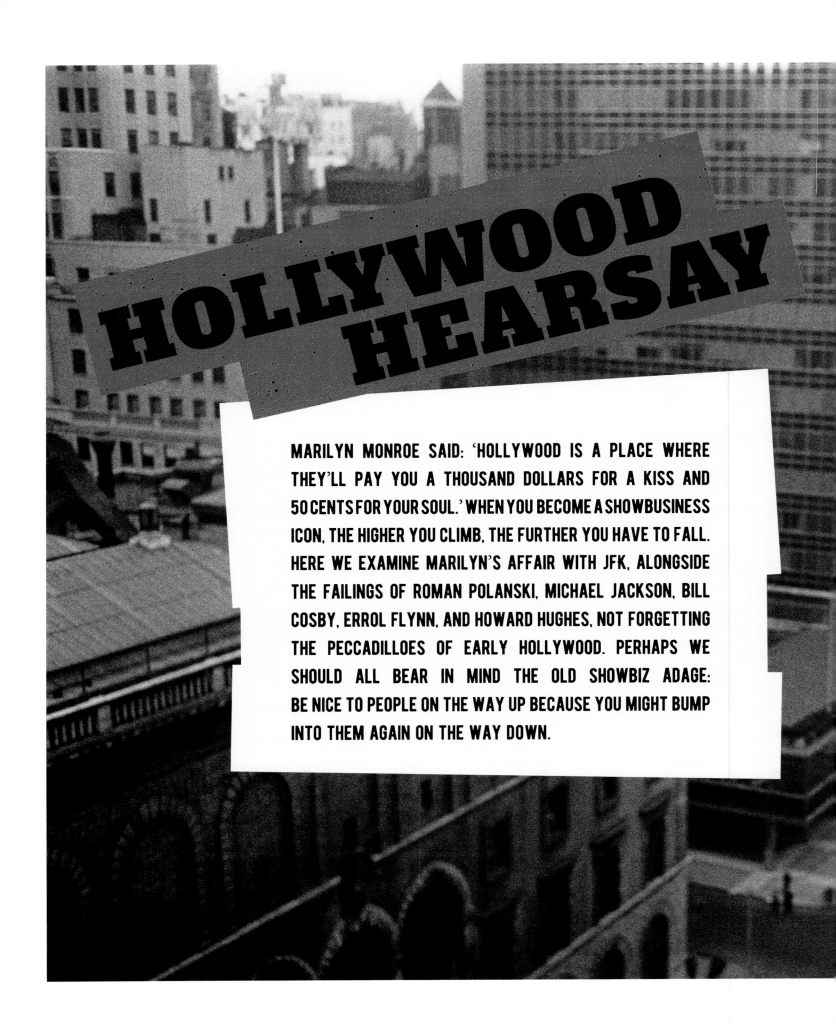

HOLLYWOOD HEARSAY

MARILYN MONROE SAID: 'HOLLYWOOD IS A PLACE WHERE THEY'LL PAY YOU A THOUSAND DOLLARS FOR A KISS AND 50 CENTS FOR YOUR SOUL.' WHEN YOU BECOME A SHOWBUSINESS ICON, THE HIGHER YOU CLIMB, THE FURTHER YOU HAVE TO FALL. HERE WE EXAMINE MARILYN'S AFFAIR WITH JFK, ALONGSIDE THE FAILINGS OF ROMAN POLANSKI, MICHAEL JACKSON, BILL COSBY, ERROL FLYNN, AND HOWARD HUGHES, NOT FORGETTING THE PECCADILLOES OF EARLY HOLLYWOOD. PERHAPS WE SHOULD ALL BEAR IN MIND THE OLD SHOWBIZ ADAGE: BE NICE TO PEOPLE ON THE WAY UP BECAUSE YOU MIGHT BUMP INTO THEM AGAIN ON THE WAY DOWN.

The fabulous Marilyn Monroe leans over the balcony at the Ambassador Hotel, New York City, in 1955.

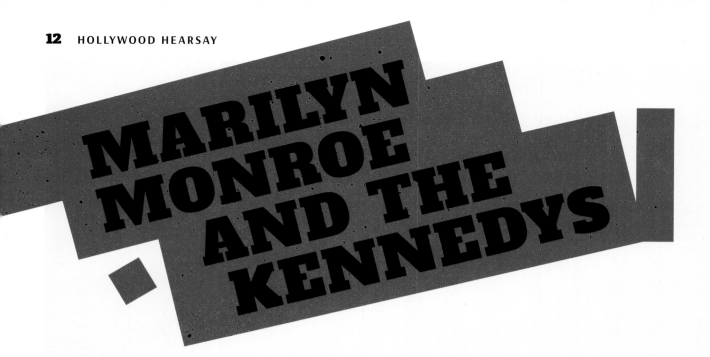

MARILYN MONROE AND THE KENNEDYS

More than five decades after his death, John Fitzgerald Kennedy remains one of America's most revered presidents. His assassination on 22 November 1963, as his motorcade passed through downtown Dallas, sent shockwaves around the world and America into a long period of mourning. Yet away from the public gaze, behind the facade of the family man with the beautiful wife and children, there was a different story to be told. President Kennedy, it would be alleged, was also a serial philanderer.

EYE FOR BEAUTY

Nobody doubted that 'Jack' Kennedy had an eye for a beautiful woman – as a single man in the late 1940s he had even dated Hollywood star Gene Tierney – but it would be more than a decade after his death before tales of his supposed infidelities began to appear in newspapers, books and magazines. By some estimates, Kennedy engaged in more than 30 extramarital flings; he is even alleged to have remarked to British prime minister Harold Macmillan: 'If I don't have sex every day, I get a headache!' Yet there was no doubting the most glamorous and celebrated of his suspected liaisons. Who else for the world's most powerful man but Hollywood's most potent symbol of female sexuality: the ultimate fantasy figure, Marilyn Monroe?

WHEN JFK MET MARILYN

Nobody knows for certain how, where or when Kennedy and Monroe met for the first time or even if they really were lovers at all. There is just one photograph in existence that shows the two of them together. The 'evidence' comes from Monroe's famous performance of 'Happy Birthday, Mr President' at a fundraiser celebration in May 1962, along with remarks made by friends and confidantes following her death. There's no question, though, that the rumours were spread well enough among Hollywood gossip columnists ... and that JFK was not the only Kennedy with whom she'd had a close relationship.

More than 50 years after her death, Marilyn Monroe is still regarded as an iconic figure of feminine beauty.

Jack Kennedy makes his inaugural speech as president, 20 January 1961.

Monroe and Kennedy were certainly on very different personal trajectories at the time they first met. At the age of 43, JFK had just sealed his rapid ascent to the peak of American politics, becoming the youngest man ever elected president. Monroe's world, on the other hand, was in freefall. In her mid-30s, her troubled private life now received more attention than her movies. After three marriages had collapsed, she suffered severe anxiety and depression and now also found herself with a spiralling drug problem. And she was about to start filming what would turn out to be her final movie project, the presciently titled *Something's Got to Give*. It would never be completed.

JFK and Marilyn Monroe were more than likely first introduced at a dinner party hosted by actor Peter Lawford in October 1961. Lawford, one of the famous 'rat pack' – along with the likes of Frank Sinatra and Sammy Davis Jr. – was married to JFK's sister Patricia, who also happened to be a close friend of Marilyn Monroe.

'HAPPY BIRTHDAY, MR PRESIDENT'

On 24 March 1962 Kennedy and Monroe were both invited to a weekend party at the Palm Springs home of Bing Crosby. According to Monroe's masseur Ralph Roberts, this was the first and only time they would sleep together. 'A great many people thought, after that weekend, that there was more to it. Marilyn gave me the impression that it was not a major event for either of them: it happened once, that weekend, and that was that,' he told Monroe's biographer, Donald Spoto.

At the Crosby party it was suggested that Monroe might perform at JFK's forthcoming fundraising gala. The event was held on 19 May 1962 and was timed to celebrate the president's forthcoming 45th birthday. In front of an audience of 15,000 at Madison Square Garden, host Peter Lawford gave Marilyn Monroe a series of comic false introductions – a running gag throughout the evening and a reference to her poor timekeeping reputation within the movie business. Finally she appeared in the spotlight and Lawford welcomed 'the late Marilyn Monroe'.

The audience gasped as she peeled off her ermine fur to reveal a figure-hugging flesh-coloured dress with more than two thousand sparkling rhinestones. In the sultriest of tones, she proceeded to sing 'Happy Birthday', inserting the words 'Mr President'. Although this had all been well choreographed, Monroe made it seem intimate, playful and off-the-cuff. President Kennedy then walked on to the stage, where he was presented with a giant birthday cake.

'I can now retire from politics,' he quickly quipped, 'after having had "Happy Birthday" sung to me in such a sweet, wholesome way.'

Such a sexually charged stage performance naturally raised eyebrows. Rumours were further fuelled when it was discovered that Kennedy's wife Jackie had not been in attendance. After the gala, celebrities gathered at the home of movie executive Arthur B. Krim and it was here that photographer Cecil Stoughton snapped the only picture of the two of them together. In spite of the frequent scandalmongering, it seems likely that this was the final occasion on which Kennedy and Monroe met.

Still wearing the flesh-coloured dress, Marilyn Monroe hangs out with Robert Kennedy (left) and JFK (right) at an aftershow party in the home of movie executive Arthur B. Krim.

'Say goodbye to Pat, say goodbye to the president, and say goodbye to yourself, because you're a nice guy.'

MARILYN MONROE

MARILYN'S BODY FOUND

In June 1962 Marilyn Monroe's personal problems escalated and her movie career collapsed. Persistent absences from the set of *Something's Got to Give* resulted in her being fired. The film's producers, 20th Century Fox, followed with a lawsuit for breach of contract. Lapsing into depression and drug abuse, she lost all interest in maintaining her appearance. At 8 p.m. on Saturday 4 August 1962, Monroe received a call from Peter Lawford at her new Hacienda-style house at 12305 Fifth Helena Drive, Los Angeles, inviting her to a party. He later recalled that she sounded drugged and had told him to: 'Say goodbye to Pat [his wife and JFK's sister], say goodbye to the president, and say goodbye to yourself, because you're a nice guy.'

In the early hours of the following morning, Marilyn Monroe's body was discovered by her housekeeper. She had died from acute barbiturate poisoning and the police had found a number of empty medicine bottles next to her bed.

The coroner's verdict put it simply: 'On more than one occasion in the past, she had made a suicide attempt, using sedative drugs. On these occasions, she had called for help and had been rescued. It is our opinion that the same pattern was repeated on the evening of Aug. 4 except for the rescue.'

WHO SHOT JFK?

At the time, Marilyn Monroe's death was regarded as a tragic suicide – just as John F. Kennedy's assassination a little over a year later was seen as a shocking murder perpetrated by a lone killer. Yet by the start of the 1980s conspiracy theories had abounded, along with a proliferation of books, articles, novels and documentaries. Was there more to these tragedies than met the eye?

The Warren Commission failed to satisfy those who believed the facts behind President Kennedy's murder were being covered up by the government. Was JFK really shot by Lee Harvey Oswald alone or was he in the employ of the CIA, who had plotted Kennedy's assassination to maintain tension with the Soviet Union following the Bay of Pigs fiasco? If not the CIA, was the Mafia involved in JFK's death or was the shooting connected with the Teamsters' president, Jimmy Hoffa? Both JFK and his younger brother, Attorney General Robert F. 'Bobby' Kennedy, had pursued Hoffa ruthlessly with allegations of corruption.

WAS IT SUICIDE?

Some also questioned whether Marilyn Monroe's death was really suicide. It was 1973's *Marilyn: A Biography* by Norman Mailer that first brought many of these ideas into the mainstream. The most widely circulated theory was that she had been killed by the CIA or the FBI as a 'point of pressure' against the Kennedy family, who were distrusted by some parts of the establishment. Interestingly, most of these theories were not connected to JFK but to her supposed affair with his brother Bobby. The bestselling biography *Goddess: The Secret Lives of Marilyn Monroe* by Anthony Summers suggested that not long before her death she'd been heavily involved with Bobby Kennedy and that when he'd ended the affair she'd threatened to tell the press.

The book implies that Kennedy and Peter Lawford prevented this by providing her with narcotics to feed her growing addiction and that she accidentally overdosed and died in an ambulance on the way to hospital. Kennedy wanted to be gone from Los Angeles by the time her death was announced, so her body was returned to her house where it was placed to look like a suicide. These claims – like all others – are still largely dismissed as fanciful speculation.

Even though more than half a century has passed, the world nevertheless remains intrigued by the story of a liaison between two of the most glamorous figures of their time and their tragically unexpected deaths. Yet in spite of the many claims made across the decades – some almost plausible, some plain crazy – perhaps the Occam's razor principle should once again be applied: the explanation requiring the least amount of speculation really is most likely to have come closest to the truth.

John F. Kennedy seated next to his wife Jacqueline at Dallas Love Field airport waiting for the cavalcade to set off for town on 22 November 1963; he was to be assassinated later that day.

ROMAN POLANSKI

A sexual assault on a child will always stir strong public feelings. And such is the nature of the crime that the perpetrator will inevitably pay a high price. If that person is a celebrity the public will rarely forgive and forget, even after a jail sentence has been served. Yet when the crime dates back to a time when sensibilities were different – and the offender is one of Hollywood's creative giants – it's clear that those rules haven't always applied.

MANSON MURDERS

Roman Polanski had already written and directed ten feature films and earned a first Oscar nomination by the time of his 30th birthday. His spectacular ascent came to a tragic halt on the night of 8–9 August 1969 when Sharon Tate, his young pregnant wife, became one of the victims in the infamous Charles Manson 'Family' murders. The horror of the unfolding events and the subsequent trial was one of the news stories of the year, the charismatic Manson earning a place among the most notorious figures in American criminal history. Overcome by grief, Polanski stepped back from the film business for several years before re-establishing himself as one of the most successful directors working in Hollywood.

SEX WITH A MINOR

At the beginning of 1977, the 44-year-old filmmaker was commissioned by French magazine *Vogue Hommes* to take a series of art photographs of adolescent girls. From the modern perspective, this concept in itself might now seem more than a little misguided – and no less so as Polanski later remarked that he'd wanted to show his subjects as 'sexy, pert, and thoroughly human'.

Polanski had been introduced to 13-year-old Samantha Gailey by her actress mother, who agreed to let him photograph her daughter privately. Gailey would later testify that she had felt uncomfortable at the initial shoot in February 1977, when Polanski asked her if she minded being photographed topless. She nevertheless agreed to join Polanski for a second session. The location was to be the luxury Mulholland Drive home of the actor Jack Nicholson, who allowed his friend to use the house while he was on a skiing vacation. Only the participants know for sure what transpired on the afternoon of 10 March 1977, but there would be life-changing repercussions for both Polanski and his subject.

According to Gailey: 'We did photos with me drinking champagne. Toward the end it got a little scary, and I realized he had other intentions.'

She later claimed that Polanski had given her a sedative, Quaalude, after which she was taken to a bedroom and sexually assaulted. Polanski later drove her home, asking her to keep their encounter secret. The girl's parents learned what had happened only after Gailey's elder sister had overheard a conversation with a friend. Polanski was arrested the following day. When questioned, he denied administering the drug and claimed that the girl had consented to the sexual activity. In his 1984 memoir, *Roman*, he merely notes that 'she wasn't unresponsive'.

Roman Polanski and his future wife Sharon Tate on the set of The Fearless Vampire Killers *(aka* Dance of the Vampires*) in 1967.*

Samantha Gailey (now Geimer) poses in front of a poster for the documentary about the scandal, which showed at the Sundance Festival in 2008. Gailey sued Polanski in 1988; the case was settled out of court.

FLIGHT TO FRANCE

Polanski received a grand jury charge covering six criminal counts, including sodomy, sex with a minor and rape by the use of drugs. To protect the young victim from the media, Gailey's attorney sought a plea bargain, asking that the felonies be replaced by the single lesser charge of unlawful sexual intercourse with a minor. At the court hearing, Polanski, dapper in a grey pinstriped suit, was asked what crime he had committed.

'I had sexual intercourse with a person not my wife, under the age of 18.'

He admitted to the judge that he had known the girl was 13 at the time. Polanski was sent to Chino State Prison for a 90-day psychiatric evaluation; a probationary sentence and deportation was the expected recommendation. The report was not unsympathetic to the film director, noting that: 'The victim was not only physically mature, but willing.' Two separate psychiatrists also assessed that he was neither a 'paedophile or sexual deviate'.

Polanski was released after 42 days, an act that angered the presiding judge, Laurence J. Rittenband, who ordered his return to jail. During this time, it was suggested to Polanski's lawyers that Judge Rittenband would now be seeking a lengthy prison sentence. Alarmed at this prospect, on 1 February 1978 Polanski bought himself a one-way flight to London, fleeing to Paris the following day. As a French citizen he would be safe from extradition to the United States. He has never returned.

NO EXTRADITION

Polanski immediately resumed his career in Europe and his work has remained popular with cinema audiences worldwide. That the industry remained firmly behind him was never in any doubt: at the 2002 Academy Awards he was given a standing ovation *in absentia* when named Best Director for his film *The Pianist*. It was only in 2018, after the Academy of

Motion Picture Arts and Sciences had established a code of conduct in the wake of the numerous sexual misconduct scandals rocking Hollywood, that Polanski was eventually expelled from the organization.

The legal ramifications would continue to follow Polanski. In 2008 his lawyers attempted to have the original case dismissed on the grounds that the original plea bargain had been violated. Judge Peter Espinoza decreed that he would only make a judgement on the case if Polanski attended court in person, but the film director refused. A year later, in September 2009, he was arrested following a US extradition demand while attempting to enter Switzerland to receive a Lifetime Achievement Award at the Zurich Film Festival. On 12 July 2010, after appeals from both the French and the Polish governments (where he had dual citizenship), the Swiss court rejected the request and Polanski was once again freed.

DEFENDED BY VICTIM

In the midst of continued controversy and claims, Samantha Gailey – by this time a married mother of three – would emerge as the unlikeliest of Polanski's defenders. She had sued in 1988, the director agreeing to a $500,000 (£383,000) settlement out of court. Since that time she has publicly forgiven him and made repeated requests for the criminal charges to be dropped. During a TV interview in 2011 she blamed the media, reporters and Judge Rittenband for causing 'way more damage to me and my family than anything Roman Polanski has ever done'. She went on to assert that, as far as she was concerned, 'his punishment was secondary to just getting this whole thing to stop'. Indeed, Gailey – now using her married name, Samantha Geimer – seems genuine in her assessment that it was this unending media aftermath that had caused the most grief in her life.

'I was a young and sexually active teenager,' she told journalists in 2017. 'I was not as traumatized as everybody thought I should have been.'

CARRY ON REGARDLESS

So what are we to make of the Polanski case? He has never denied his wrongdoing, even telling author Martin Amis during a 1979 interview that everyone wanted to have sex with young girls. Yet there remains an abiding sense that while he may have been unable to return to the United States, Polanski has been able to continue with his life and career largely unhindered. And this begs questions that have come increasingly into focus in recent times, not the least of which is how we are supposed to separate the personal lives of artists from their works. Many have been critical of the way in which Polanski has been afforded such a smooth ride by both critics and cinema audiences – more so since further (as yet unsubstantiated) allegations of sexual abuse have come to light over the past decade.

There is little doubt that had this crime been committed more recently, Roman Polanski would not only have been incarcerated for a very long term, but would also have been reviled within the film industry. Yet while he undeniably broke the law, not only has he been able to evade justice for more than four decades but he has also continued – even well into his eighties – as a commercially successful filmmaker, his reputation as one of cinema's auteurs largely unblemished.

THE RISE AND FALL OF AMERICA'S FATHER FIGURE

It's always troubling when a much-loved figure fails to live up to the expectations of their public image. Not only had Bill Cosby enjoyed a 50-year career as one of America's most popular entertainers, but he was an influential figure to several generations of African Americans. His impressive achievements are many.

NATIONAL TREASURE

A three-times Emmy winner in the mid-1960s action series *I Spy*, Cosby was the first black actor to star in a popular drama show. At the same time he was performing groundbreaking stand-up comedy to stadium audiences and producing bestselling albums. His greatest success came in the 1980s with *The Cosby Show,* a family sitcom that made him a household name. With Cosby portraying the kindly, wholesome, jumper-wearing Cliff Huxtable – a wealthy, educated, upper-middle-class black doctor – it was not only the country's most popular TV show for five consecutive seasons but it also received universal praise for providing a positive image of a modern black American family. As 'America's Dad', Bill Cosby was a national treasure.

As with many celebrity sex scandals, while the lurid details were unknown to the public at large, rumour and accusation regarding Cosby's private life had been in circulation for many years; details of alleged sexual assaults were certainly reported to journalists as early as 1980, even if none of this was ever published at the time.

DRUGGED AND ASSAULTED

It wasn't until 2000 that a formal criminal complaint was first filed against Cosby. His accuser was Lachele Covington, a 20-year-old aspiring actress, who had asked the actor for career advice. After a dinner date she was invited to his home where she claimed that Cosby

groped her breasts and attempted to put his hands down her pants. Covington reported the matter to the police, but no prosecution was brought.

It was in January 2005 that former professional basketball player Andrea Constand first approached the police after her own experience with Bill Cosby. They had first met three years earlier, when Constand was operations director of Temple University's women's basketball team. As a Temple alumnus of the early sixties, Cosby had maintained strong ties with his alma mater and he followed its sports teams avidly. Over the next two years Constand would often attend dinner parties at Cosby's mansion in suburban Philadelphia.

In January 2004, Constand visited Cosby's house after a night out with some friends. She alleged that after she had asked him for advice on dealing with stress, Cosby gave her three blue pills that he claimed would help her relax. 'Your friends,' he called them. According to her testimony, Constand was rendered barely conscious and unable to move, during which time Cosby fondled her breasts, penetrated her with his fingers and placed her hand on his genitals. When she awoke at 4 a.m. she found her clothing strewn across the room.

It was some months later, after Constand had described the assault to her mother, that she sought legal action. In January 2005 a criminal investigation was opened by Pennsylvania detectives. When questioned about the incident, Cosby claimed that sex was consensual and that the pills were merely antihistamines, available over the counter in any drug store. On 22 February, District Attorney Bruce Castor decided that 'insufficient credible

Surrounded by a phalanx of police officers, actor and stand-up Bill Cosby shows the strain as he leaves Montgomery Courthouse after the sixth day of his retrial on serious sexual assault charges, 16 April 2018. At least 60 women have accused the 80-year-old of impropriety.

and admissible evidence exists upon which any charge against Mr. Cosby could be sustained beyond reasonable doubt'. The case was taken no further.

Constand nevertheless continued to pursue Cosby and in March 2005 she filed a civil claim against the actor. By this time it had become clear that her experience was not unique; a dozen other women had also agreed to present similar testimonies should the matter come to court. In a private legal deposition that would later play a key role in his prosecution, under oath Cosby denied ever sexually assaulting any woman, but made the shocking disclosure that he had obtained Quaalude sedatives from a gynaecologist to administer – illegally – to young women prior to sex. In November 2006 Cosby agreed on an undisclosed settlement (later reported as $3.38m/£2.59m), with both parties signing a confidentiality agreement.

FURTHER ALLEGATIONS

Allegations against Cosby soon began to seep into the tabloid media, for whom the lurid 'Dr Huxtable & Mr Hyde' stories were irresistible. Cosby remained silent throughout and his public remained loyal. It wasn't until the era of social media that this trickle of allegations began to proliferate.

In October 2014, comedian Hannibal Buress began a routine built around Bill Cosby's well-publicized negative moralizing about young black men and their lifestyles.

'But you raped women, Bill Cosby, so that kind of brings you down a couple notches.'

The experiences they described were eerily familiar – sedation followed by sexual assault.

A video clip of the segment – in which Buress also implored the audibly shocked audience to 'Google Bill Cosby rape' – went viral. The floodgates opened and in quick succession more than two dozen women – among them models Janice Dickinson and Beverly Johnson and actresses Louisa Moritz and Michelle Hurd – would make their own accusations public. The experiences they described were eerily familiar – sedation followed by sexual assault, the earliest incident going back as far as 1965.

Cosby could no longer ignore what was fast becoming a PR disaster. Through his attorney he would make frequent pronouncements, rubbishing individual accounts, denying any wrongdoing, dismissing allegations as unsubstantiated and finally lambasting what he described as 'media vilification'. These public statements led Andrea Constand to file a motion negating their confidentiality agreement, her attorney arguing that Cosby had already effectively done so through his responses in the media. The judge ruled in her favour, declaring that Cosby's 2005 deposition could be made public.

In spite of complaints from Cosby's lawyers, who claimed that he 'admitted to nothing more than being one of the many people who introduced Quaaludes into their consensual sex life in the 1970s', on 30 December 2015 Bill Cosby was arrested and charged with three counts of aggravated indecent assault on Andrea Constand. After appeals to have the case dismissed failed, a trial date of 5 June 2017 was set.

TRIAL AND SENTENCING

In his opening statement, Assistant District Attorney Kristen Feden told jurors that when Cosby 'handed those pills to Andrea he knew what effect it would take ... this is a case about a man who used his power and his fame and his previously practiced method of placing a young trusting woman in an incapacitated state so that he could sexually pleasure himself so that she couldn't say no.'

The trial itself was short, but after five days and 52 hours of deliberation – longer than the defence and prosecution had spent on their presentations – the jury was unable to reach a unanimous verdict. A mistrial was declared and the retrial took place ten months later. This time, on 26 April 2018, Bill Cosby was found guilty on all three counts of indecent assault.

The three felonies were each punishable by up to ten years in prison and a $25,000 (£19,000) fine. At his sentencing on 26 September 2018, Cosby was given a jail term of three-to-ten – between three and ten years. After denying a request that he remain free on bail while pursuing an appeal, Judge Steven T. O'Neill declared: 'This was a serious crime ... Mr Cosby, this has all circled back to you. The day has come. The time has come.' Cosby was led out of court in handcuffs.

By the time of sentencing, 60 women had come forward with similar stories. As former model Jewel Allison – another of Cosby's accusers – remarked: 'He got away with it because he was hiding behind the image of Cliff Huxtable.'

A job well done: flanked by prosecutors, Andrea Constand reacts to the guilty verdict for Bill Cosby on all three counts of sexual assault, 26 April 2018.

THE KING OF POP LOSES HIS CROWN

Michael Jackson, the 'King of Pop', was one of the most celebrated stars ever to have lived. Famous from the age of 11, not only did he score more than 70 hits over the course of four decades, but he created *Thriller*, one of the most commercially successful albums in history. Yet in the end his unique talents would be eclipsed by his bizarre lifestyle as he became mired in rumours and allegations of sexual assaults on minors.

ECCENTRIC STAR

Bubbles was Michael Jackson's pet chimpanzee and they regularly wore matching outfits.

Michael Jackson was the eighth of ten siblings, all raised to be performers by their ambitious and tyrannical father. At an age when most children were still in elementary school, Jackson's days were spent in television studios and on gruelling tours with his brothers in The Jackson 5. By his late teens, Jackson was already a pop veteran, with dozens of hits behind him and now a rapidly flourishing solo career. Less than a decade later, in the middle of the 1980s, Jackson was the biggest-selling artist on the planet.

Yet as his career reached ever new heights so his behaviour in public became increasingly eccentric. He was often seen accompanied by Bubbles, a chimpanzee which lived in a crib in Jackson's bedroom. Jackson and the chimp could regularly be seen wearing matching costumes. He was also reported to have become obsessed with the story of Joseph Merrick, 'The Elephant Man', so much so that he attempted to buy his deformed skeleton from a London hospital. Over time, plastic surgery altered his facial features

Michael Jackson in Los Angeles for the Grammys in 1984: it was the year of Thriller *and he walked away with a record-breaking eight awards.*

and, most dramatically, his skin began to lighten. Jackson claimed it was a pigmentation disorder called vitiligo, but rumours circulated that it was a result of deliberate bleaching.

Then there was Neverland. A 3,000-acre ranch bought in 1988, Jackson renamed it after the fantasy island to which Peter Pan escaped in order to live his eternal childhood. As well as being Jackson's home, it was also a private amusement park, complete with Ferris wheel, roller coasters, bumper cars and an arcade. Unsurprisingly, many commentators viewed Neverland as symbolizing Jackson's lost childhood.

MISSING GIRLFRIEND?

Particularly unusual for one of America's wealthiest young men, however, was that throughout his twenties Jackson had lacked a publicly visible girlfriend. This led to inevitable speculation about his sexuality.

Matters took a very dark turn in 1993. Jackson had become friendly with the family of 13-year-old Jordan Chandler, who had often taken part in sleepovers at Neverland. Chandler's father then alleged that his son had been sexually assaulted on more than one occasion and sought a private settlement from the singer. When his $20 million (£15.3m) demand was refused, Chandler went to the police. In August 1993 the LAPD raided Neverland and books and photographs were seized. The child told the police that a sexual relationship had taken place that included kissing, masturbation and oral sex. Four months later, Jackson was served with a warrant for a strip search: Chandler had evidently described intimate parts of Jackson's anatomy. However, the investigation was ultimately deemed inconclusive and no charges were brought. Nevertheless, in the middle of his mammoth 18-month Dangerous World Tour Jackson was under commercial pressure to limit PR damage, so he paid the Chandler family $23 million (£17.6m) and made a public statement declaring his innocence.

'It was the most humiliating ordeal of my life, one that no person should ever have to suffer ... but if this is what I have to endure to prove my innocence, my complete innocence, so be it.'

Jackson and friends attend the Dangerous World Tour press conference in New York, 1992.

FATHERHOOD

Although Jackson was not charged, many of the newspaper headlines nonetheless implied his guilt. Further stories began emerging of close friendships with young boys, among them child star Macaulay Culkin. Although magazine polls taken at the time suggested that a majority of people believed Jackson was being unjustly persecuted, the Chandler case would damage his career and exacerbate a prescription drug problem that would last throughout his life.

As an artist, Michael Jackson might now have been in commercial decline, but he was still able to ship 20 million copies of his 1995 album *HIStory*. At the same time, his public displays of eccentricity grew ever more frequent and erratic. Eyebrows were raised in 1994 when he married Priscilla Presley, the daughter of Elvis. There were tabloid suggestions that this was a cynical stunt to rehabilitate his image and the marriage ended two years later in divorce. He then married nurse Debbie Rowe. When their two children, Michael 'Prince' Jr. and Paris-Michael were born, the tabloids were again filled with speculation – this time they were saying that his wife was little more than a surrogate. When they divorced in 1999 she received a hefty payment and Jackson received full custodial rights.

INCRIMINATING EVIDENCE

After the Chandler affair there would be persistent rumours about the questionable amount of time Jackson had spent in the company of young boys. This became news once again in 2003 when the television documentary *Living with Michael Jackson* was broadcast. During eight days spent filming with British journalist Martin Bashir, the singer's bizarre behaviour was exhibited to the full. The film crew was there when he infamously presented his infant son Prince to fans and photographers by dangling him dangerously over the railings of a fourth-floor hotel balcony. He was also filmed on several of his mind-boggling, high-speed, multi-million-dollar shopping sprees in Las Vegas. But the following day's tabloid headlines literally composed themselves the moment Jackson told Bashir that he often shared his bedroom with his young 'friends':

Jackson dangles his eight-month-old son Prince from the balcony of the Adlon Hotel, Berlin, 2002.

filmed holding hands with the singer was 12-year-old Gavin Arvizo, a young cancer survivor who had spent many nights at Neverland. When challenged by Bashir, Jackson responded: 'It's not sexual; we're going to sleep.' He seemed to have no understanding that anyone would think otherwise.

Thirty-eight million Americans watched the two-hour documentary and the media were quick to condemn Jackson in the days that followed. The singer claimed that Bashir had created a distorted picture of his behaviour, causing him to feel betrayed. The controversy nevertheless aroused the suspicions of the authorities and after an investigation by the LAPD, on 18 December 2003 Jackson was indicted on seven counts of child molestation in the case of Gavin Arvizo, and two further counts of intoxicating his victim.

VINDICATED BY COURT

The People of the State of California v. Michael Joe Jackson began on 28 February 2005. Every day of the sensational trial would be eagerly devoured by the world's media. Jackson's legal team went on the immediate offence, describing the child's mother as a 'con artist' who used her cancer-stricken son to prey on celebrities. Yet the evidence from Arvizo seemed damning. He claimed that Jackson had masturbated him while they were in his bed and had given him wine – or 'Jesus Juice', as Jackson was alleged to have called it. But his testimony was gravely undermined by having told his schoolteacher that he had not been molested, though Arvizo claimed that he'd said this only in an effort to end teasing from his classmates. Evidence from the LAPD revealed that during their search of Neverland many sexually explicit magazines and DVDs had been discovered but, critically, there was no evidence to suggest that Jackson had shown them to the child. After 30 hours of deliberation, on 13 June 2005 the jury reached a verdict: not guilty on all counts.

The news of Jackson's death created a global frenzy and brought the Internet grinding to a halt.

In the aftermath, Michael Jackson would leave America for Bahrain. He may have been vindicated in the courts, but the world's tabloid media jury was still out and the trickle of negative publicity carried on unabated. Jackson maintained a low profile over the next four years until March 2009, when he announced a series of ten comeback concerts at London's O2 Arena. Over a million tickets were sold in less than two hours, leading to the record-breaking run being increased to 50 shows, to commence on 13 July 2009.

CARDIAC ARREST

But the concerts never took place. On 25 June 2009 Michael Jackson died from a cardiac arrest brought about by acute propofol and benzodiazepine intoxication. (His personal physician, Dr Conrad Murray, was later convicted of involuntary manslaughter.) The news of Jackson's death created a global frenzy and brought the Internet grinding to a halt. The outpouring of grief that followed, including the live television broadcast of his funeral, was living proof that millions of fans the world over had remained loyal. Indeed, his estate continues to receive astronomical global royalties – in 2016 alone, *Forbes* estimated his earnings to be $825 million (£633m), the largest ever recorded for a dead celebrity.

NEW EVIDENCE

Questions about the true nature of Jackson's relationship with his 'young friends' continue to the present day. In 2019, a controversial documentary, *Leaving Neverland*, was first shown in the US and then in the UK, despite the efforts of the Jackson estate to have it pulled. It focussed on two of Jackson's alleged victims, James Safechuck and Wade Robson. Safechuck, now aged 41, first met Jackson when he appeared in a Pepsi advertisement with him at the age of ten and maintains he was sexually abused by the singer from then onwards.

Thirty-six-year-old Robson claims to have been abused by the singer between the ages of seven and 14. Although both of them defended Jackson in court in 1993, they would now change their stories, saying that only now were they able to speak about their childhood ordeals.

From Beauty to Beast: Michael Jackson leaves the Santa Barbara County Courthouse where he was being tried on child molestation charges, 2005.

As Martin Bashir himself pointed out following Michael Jackson's death, the singer was 'never convicted of any crime'. Yet as the damning allegations continue to be aired, we're forced to ask the same dreadful question: was Michael Jackson a paedophile?

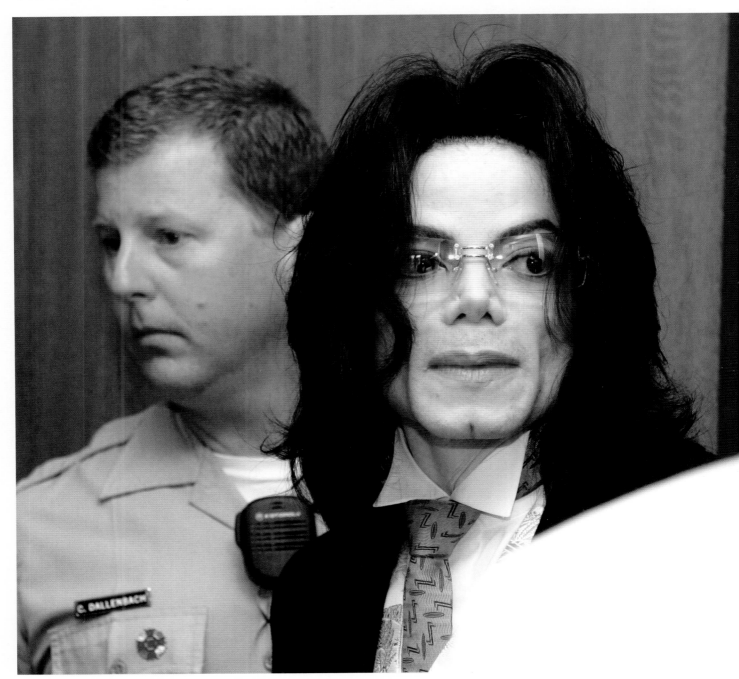

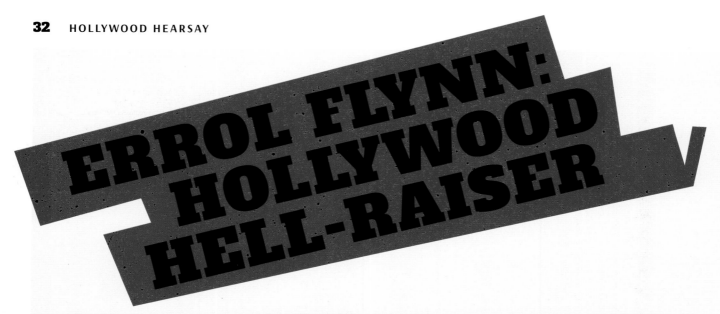

ERROL FLYNN: HOLLYWOOD HELL-RAISER

He was the swashbuckling hero of Hollywood, an impossibly handsome man of action no woman could resist – a hard-drinking hell-raiser who was envied by every young man. The tales of Errol Flynn's voracious sexual appetite were of such legend that the phrase 'In like Flynn!' entered the English language. In the end, it would also be his undoing.

OVERNIGHT SUCCESS

Errol Flynn's acting career began as something of an accident. Born into a wealthy family in Tasmania, after an undistinguished educational record Flynn spent his early twenties working in the tobacco and metal mining industries. At the age of 24 he was spotted by Australian filmmaker Charles Chauvel, who was looking for a handsome young man to play the role of Fletcher Christian in a 1933 movie called *In the Wake of the Bounty*. The film was unsuccessful, but Flynn, the ever-restless chancer, saw it as a possible route to fame and fortune. He then made his way to London, where in 1934 his looks earned him a role in Warner Brothers' crime thriller *Murder at Monte Carlo*. Impressed with his on-screen charisma, the studio signed him up to a contract and sent him off to Hollywood, where he became an overnight hit. His first starring role, in swashbuckling pirate movie *Captain Blood*, was box office gold. Hit after hit followed – including *The Charge of the Light Brigade* and *The Adventures of Robin Hood* – and by 1940 he was one of Hollywood's most popular romantic leads.

As with many stars of the period, Warner Brothers cultivated a very deliberate screen image for Flynn, designed to appeal to both young men and women. He was the strong, daring, elegant, debonair romantic – sometimes a little shy; sometimes a little rakish – but his leading lady would inevitably bring out a softer, vulnerable side. This was in stark contrast to the real Errol Flynn.

RAPE CHARGES

Flynn's drinking was almost as legendary within Hollywood as his sexual conquests. 'I like my whisky old and my women young,' the actor would utter on more than one occasion. The parties he threw with close friend David Niven were so riotous that the villa they shared was dubbed 'Cirrhosis-by-the-Sea'. Stories of his overindulgence took on a mythological status, as did the supposed size of his appendage. In his book *Music for Chameleons*, Truman Capote relates a story told by Marilyn Monroe

Man in tights: Errol Flynn poses for a publicity still for The Adventures of Robin Hood, *1958, directed by Michael Curtiz.*

Nightclub dancer Peggy Satterlee (left), wearing youthful pigtails and jumper, prepares to tell the court about her relations with actor Errol Flynn. Betty Hansen (right) tells the court about her dealings with Flynn to much laughter from a packed courtroom.

about a drunken party she attended, where Flynn had played tunes on the piano using his penis!

Long the subject of the Hollywood gossip columnists – whom Flynn would frequently confront in person – the high jinks turned very sour in January 1943. In a Los Angeles courtroom, Errol Flynn was charged with two counts of statutory rape.

At a party the previous September, Flynn had been introduced to 17-year-old starlet Betty Hansen.

In court she testified that she consumed so much alcohol at the party that she vomited. Flynn took her upstairs to a bathroom so she could clean herself up, after which, she claimed, he seduced her in a bedroom. Flynn denied any impropriety.

'I'm bewildered,' the actor responded. 'I barely touched her.'

The second charge was brought by Peggy Satterlee, also 17 years old, who claimed he had 'taken advantage' of her during a trip to Catalina Island on his private yacht, *Sirocco*. She testified that Flynn had entered her cabin and 'got into bed with me and completed an act of sexual intercourse'. She admitted that she did not struggle. The same thing happened the following night, only this time it was claimed that she had tried to fend him off. The prosecution argued that since Flynn had nicknamed her 'J.B.' (standing for 'jail bait') he must have been aware that she was a juvenile – the age of consent in California being 18 years. Again, Flynn denied the charge.

ACQUITTAL

Ace Hollywood lawyer Jerry Geisler was hired to defend the 33-year-old film star and private investigators searched into the backgrounds of the young women. Hansen, whose testimony had sometimes been confused and contradictory, was shown to be awaiting trial on a felony charge, so Geisler told the court her statements were unreliable. He took a similar line of questioning with Satterlee: under cross-examination she admitted that she had often lied about her age, had previously had an affair with a married man and had also undergone an abortion – illegal in the United States at the time.

The jury of nine women and three men deliberated for 13 hours before returning a verdict of not guilty. After the trial, jury foreman Ruby Anderson spoke to the press: 'We felt there had been other men in the girls' lives. Frankly, the cards were on the table and we couldn't believe the girls' stories.'

GONE BEFORE HIS TIME

Although he was acquitted of any wrongdoing, the trial's widespread coverage not only severely damaged Errol Flynn's career, but it was also responsible for creating a wider media fascination with the private lives of Hollywood's superstars. More than 70 years later, that interest shows few signs of easing.

By the end of the 1940s, hard living, alcohol, drugs and general self-indulgence had taken their toll on Flynn's health and appearance. No longer a leading man or a box office draw, Flynn tried his luck briefly in Europe before returning to Hollywood, where he died in 1959 at the age of 50. With him was his final young conquest, 17-year-old actress Beverly Aadland.

After Flynn's death it was alleged by her mother that she had been 15 when their relationship had first begun. The coroner's report listed cirrhosis and fatty generation of the liver as being among the many lifestyle factors that had contributed to his premature death. As Flynn himself had once wryly remarked: 'My problem lies with reconciling my gross habits with my net income.'

By the end of the 1940s, hard living, alcohol, drugs and general self-indulgence had taken their toll on Flynn's health and appearance.

Long before the Harvey Weinstein allegations and the #MeToo movement, there was Howard Hughes, one of the world's wealthiest men. A legendary playboy and powerful studio owner, he used his position as one of the biggest Hollywood producers of the 1940s and 1950s to seduce some of its biggest stars.

BORN TO WEALTH

Hughes was born in 1905 into immense wealth. His father had been a successful inventor who patented a drill that revolutionized the oil industry. When Hughes was 18 his father died suddenly, leaving him millions of dollars and a thriving business. The young Hughes then dropped out of university to pursue the three great loves of his life: flying, movies ... and women.

He started out in Hollywood producing silent comedies and gangster films. A couple of those were financially successful, but he first made his mark in 1930 by producing and directing *Hell's Angels*, a spectacular action yarn about pilots in the First World War. Featuring lengthy, epic live-action dogfight scenes, the film cost $4 million (£3.1 million) to produce and was notable as the most expensive movie ever made at that time.

By the 1940s, Hughes was one of the most successful independent producers working in Hollywood, and later bought the famous RKO studios for cash. Although he no longer directed his films, he exerted a huge influence over the way they were made and in particular the manner in which his leading ladies were portrayed on screen. Frequently at odds with censors at the Hays Office, Hughes constantly edged back the boundaries of acceptability, presenting a succession of sexually charged female fantasy figures. One notable controversy surrounded *The Outlaw*, a western based on the life of Billy the Kid. It involved star actress Jane Russell – or more particularly the way in which the camera spent so much of the film's 116 minutes trained on her breasts. The Hays censors refused to certify the movie without cuts being made, declaring that Russell's body had been 'shockingly emphasized'. (A fact Hughes could hardly argue with since he had personally designed the bra worn by Russell in the film!)

THE LEADING LADIES

As Hughes aged so the lines between his professional and personal relationships would become progressively blurred, and he developed increasingly obsessional behaviour towards his leading ladies. The story was much the same as many of those heard half a century later during the #MeToo scandals. Hughes would use his position to exploit any woman that took his fancy – and not only starlets looking for a way into the movies.

He wielded his power to bed many of the greatest stars of Hollywood's Golden Age – the likes of Bette Davis, Ginger Rogers, Lana Turner, Jean Harlow, Katharine Hepburn and Rita Hayworth.

He even dated Olivia de Havilland and Joan Fontaine – who were sisters – at the same time. His sexual appetite led Joan Crawford to note caustically that: 'Howard Hughes would f··k a tree!'

The most significant of Hughes' many relationships was with movie superstar Ava Gardner. Divorced in 1943 from actor Mickey Rooney, she provided a revealing glimpse into his attitudes.

Howard Hughes with Ava Gardner at a boxing match in New York. Hughes was recovering from injuries sustained in a plane crash.

'He had people meeting every plane, train and bus that arrived in Los Angeles with a pretty girl on board,' she remarked. 'He had to be the first to grab the new girl in town. When he read the story of my divorce in the papers, he decided I was the new girl on the loose.'

Their torrid on–off affair sometimes descended into physical abuse towards one another. During one violent clash Hughes punched her in the face, dislocating her jaw, and she responded by smashed an ashtray over his head, knocking him unconscious. Fearing she had killed him, Gardner called MGM boss Louis Mayer, who sent over one of his fixers to deal with the situation. She recalled that it was she who was given the stern rebuke by the studio head for striking Hughes. There was no criticism of him.

Jane Russell in a still from the film The Outlaw, *1941.*

There was a more sinister, controlling side to the way Hughes viewed his actresses, and he wasn't above dealing out vindictive retribution to those who rebuffed his advances. Jane Greer, a popular screen femme fatale contracted to RKO Pictures, was one of his victims. She recalled his fury at being turned down. 'As long as I own this studio you won't work,' he shouted. A promising career was stalled overnight. 'I was stuck dead in my tracks,' she noted years later.

THE RECLUSE

By 1960, Howard Hughes had left the movie world behind. Through his business interests in aviation and real estate he was one of the richest men in the world, but he was also displaying increasingly compulsive and eccentric behaviour, eating identical meals each day and refusing to bathe or cut his hair or nails. On Thanksgiving Day 1966 he rented the top two floors of the Desert Inn hotel and casino in Las Vegas, but as neither Hughes nor his employees gambled he was asked to leave ten days later. His response was to buy the 300-room hotel. Thereafter he lived the life of a recluse, making business deals from the penthouse suite he never left, the curtains always drawn, the windows and doors sealed with tape.

It has been said, in the light of some of the older #MeToo allegations, that standards for acceptable behaviour can't necessarily be applied in the same way to past eras. Howard Hughes may have been exploitative when it came to actresses, but it's doubtful that he would have been regarded as ever having committed a serious crime. In the end, the way he viewed women was perhaps little different from many other powerful male figures of his generation. The continual stream of present-day #MeToo allegations would seem to suggest that some of these attitudes remain hard-wired in Hollywood.

Reclusive billionaire Howard Hughes in a 1947 photo (left) and in 1972 (right). Doubts have been raised as to whether the later image, taken in Vancouver, was even Hughes at all.

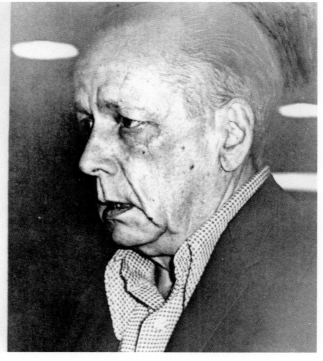

SEX AND THE SILENT ERA

It's hard to imagine that Hollywood, for more than a century the epicentre of the cinema world, barely existed before the moviemakers arrived. In 1900 the population stood at barely 500 and the roads and pavements were still gravel. At this time, movie patents were held by Thomas Edison's Motion Picture Company on the East Coast, so early filmmakers began migrating to southern California where the patents were not always legally enforced by the courts. The Los Angeles suburb proved an ideal location. Land was cheap, the weather was perfect for filming and the mountains, deserts and plains provided an ideal backdrop for outdoor adventure movies. And it would soon be home to many of America's most notorious sex scandals.

WRONGLY ACCUSED

At the height of Hollywood's silent era, comedy actor Roscoe 'Fatty' Arbuckle was Paramount Pictures' prize asset. Early in 1921, the 266-lb (19-stone) comedian, billed as 'worth his weight in laughs', signed Hollywood's first-ever million-dollar deal. While he was hosting a party in his hotel room on 5 September 1921, one of his guests, aspiring young actress Virginia Rappe, became seriously ill – most likely from chronic cystitis aggravated by poor-quality Prohibition-era bootleg alcohol. Four days later she died of a ruptured bladder. Her friend Bambina Delmont, who had also attended the party, claimed that she had been raped by Arbuckle. Doctors found no such evidence but the police pursued Arbuckle, declaring that his enormous body on top of the actress was the cause of the rupture. Rappe's manager claimed in the press that she had been penetrated by a piece of ice to simulate sex, but witnesses at the party maintained that Arbuckle had rubbed ice on her abdomen to relieve the pain.

Ultimately the prosecutor could find no evidence of rape, but he nonetheless filed charges of manslaughter. After two mistrials, Arbuckle was found not guilty. The jury statement went further: 'Acquittal is not enough for Roscoe Arbuckle. We feel that a great injustice has been done him ... The happening at the hotel was an unfortunate affair for which Arbuckle, so the evidence shows, was in no way responsible.'

View of the courtroom where Roscoe 'Fatty' Arbuckle can be seen seated right in the centre of the image.

Virginia Rappe, who died following a party at Fatty Arbuckle's suite at a San Francisco hotel.

Unfortunately for Arbuckle, he had endured nine months of vilification in the press by the time of his third trial and his work had been banned from cinemas – indeed, many of his films from the early 1920s were destroyed and are now forever lost. In spite of his innocence, Roscoe Arbuckle was effectively blacklisted for the rest of the decade and was only able to work under assumed names. Arbuckle died following a heart attack on 29 June 1933 – the day after he signed a contract to star in what should have been his Hollywood comeback. He was just 46 years old.

The case was certainly monumental for the US media, illustrating for the first time the effectiveness of exaggerating and sensationalizing a sex scandal to sell newspapers. William Randolph Hearst, America's first newspaper mogul, quipped that the Arbuckle scandal 'sold more newspapers than any event since the sinking of the *Lusitania*'.

HOLLYWOOD'S FIRST SCANDAL

The Roscoe Arbuckle trial may have captured the news headlines, but it was only one of a number of scandals that hit the Paramount Pictures studios at around the same time. A year earlier, in 1920, film beauty Olive Thomas died in mysterious circumstances while holidaying in Paris with her actor husband Jack Pickford. She evidently drank from a flask that she thought was water but actually contained mercury bichloride prescribed for her husband's chronic syphilis. She was rushed to hospital, but in the five days before she died rumours began to appear in the press that she had attempted suicide after discovering that she had been given syphilis by Pickford. Another story had it that she and her husband were debauched drug addicts. Pickford denied everything, calling the whole business a 'ghastly mistake', and the Paris physician who examined her ruled her death as accidental. The Thomas case has been described as Hollywood's first scandal. It was certainly the first instance of media sensationalism related to a major film star.

DRUGS AND MURDER

The death of Paramount film director William Desmond Taylor not only provided Hollywood's first drug scandal but also its first murder mystery. And, of course, sex also played its part. On the morning of 2 February 1922, Taylor was found shot dead inside his Los Angeles bungalow. No weapon was found on the scene, although in his possession was a large amount of cash, a two-carat diamond ring and a locket bearing a photograph of popular comedy actress Mabel

Normand. So robbery was clearly not the motive. The press leapt on the story when the police investigation revealed that Normand was a cocaine addict who had sought help from Taylor. The director had subsequently fallen in love with the actress and become obsessed by her. Shortly before his murder, Taylor had offered to help federal prosecutors apprehend Normand's cocaine supplier and it was widely believed that he was a victim of a contract killer hired by the drug dealers. During the police investigation, physical evidence from the crime scene vanished mysteriously and 40 years later retired police officer William Cahill told an interviewer that although they had been making progress they suddenly 'got the word to lay off'.

Minter's reputation as the wholesome young girl she portrayed in her films was shattered.

RELATIONSHIP WITH CHILD STAR

There was significant collateral damage surrounding the Taylor case. After the reports of her drug use, Mabel Normand's film career was ruined. When the police searched Taylor's home they also found passionate love letters written to him by child star Mary Miles Minter, whom he had directed in the 1919 movie hit *Anne of Green Gables*. At a time when there were more than a few corrupt Los Angeles police officers in the pockets of the press, the letters found their way into the hands of reporters. Newspapers were soon filled with allegations of a sexual relationship between the 49-year-old director and the 17-year-old starlet. Minter's reputation as the wholesome young girl she portrayed in her films was shattered and soon afterwards she retired from the film business.

The murder of William Desmond Taylor was never solved, although among the leading suspects had been former actress Charlotte Shelby, the mother of Mary Miles Minter, who owned a gun matching that used in the murder. There was a curious final twist to the mystery in 1964, when Margaret Gibson, an actress who had appeared in a number of films, made a deathbed confession to Taylor's murder. She had been arrested in connection with a blackmail and extortion ring in the early 1920s.

BIRTH OF THE HAYS CODE

These early Hollywood scandals had a massive impact on the film industry. Studio heads realized for the first time that the way their stars behaved in private could have a direct impact on profits, so they began to introduce morality clauses into performers' contracts. At the same time religious groups branded Hollywood as a corrupt and damaging influence on young America and began lobbying politicians to take action. By the beginning of 1922, almost 100 cinema censorship bills were being introduced by legislators in 37 different states. In an attempt to avoid having to comply with a raft of potential new legislation, the industry came together and Postmaster General and Presbyterian elder Will H. Hays was enlisted to rehabilitate Hollywood's image. This would eventually result in the Motion Picture Production Code (or the 'Hays Code'), a set of guidelines that would place restrictions on what could be shown in films over the three decades that followed.

Finally, of course, it taught the media one of its most enduring lessons. That sex sells.

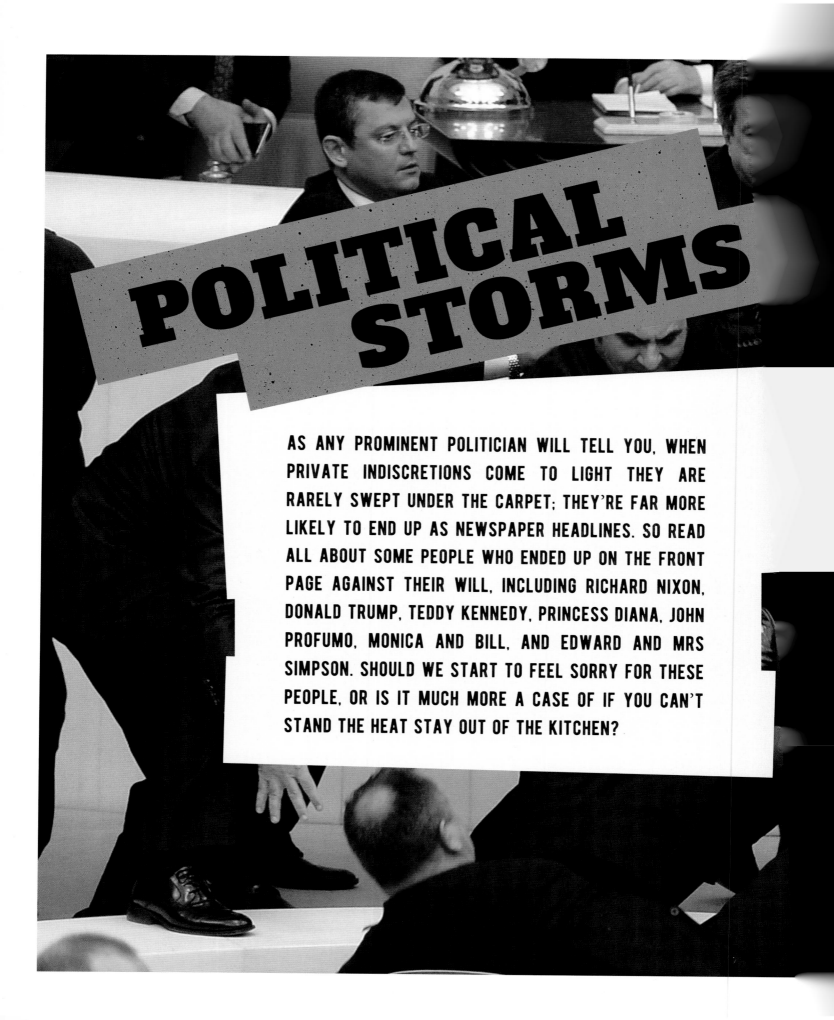

POLITICAL STORMS

AS ANY PROMINENT POLITICIAN WILL TELL YOU, WHEN PRIVATE INDISCRETIONS COME TO LIGHT THEY ARE RARELY SWEPT UNDER THE CARPET; THEY'RE FAR MORE LIKELY TO END UP AS NEWSPAPER HEADLINES. SO READ ALL ABOUT SOME PEOPLE WHO ENDED UP ON THE FRONT PAGE AGAINST THEIR WILL, INCLUDING RICHARD NIXON, DONALD TRUMP, TEDDY KENNEDY, PRINCESS DIANA, JOHN PROFUMO, MONICA AND BILL, AND EDWARD AND MRS SIMPSON. SHOULD WE START TO FEEL SORRY FOR THESE PEOPLE, OR IS IT MUCH MORE A CASE OF IF YOU CAN'T STAND THE HEAT STAY OUT OF THE KITCHEN?

They like a good fight in the Turkish parliament; this one took place on 12 February 2015.

The war in Vietnam had been painful for America. For one, the nation's reputation as an unequivocal force for good had been compromised in the eyes of the world. And back home a deeply divided country debated the rights and wrongs of the conflict – the first time that a large portion of the population had found itself violently at odds with its government's foreign policy.

NIXON ON THE ATTACK

In 1972, President Richard M. Nixon faced his own battle for re-election and Vietnam was at the very heart of his campaign. The Republican Nixon administration attacked the opposing candidate, Senator George McGovern, as a weak liberal who, they claimed, supported abortion rights, was soft on drugs and would offer amnesties to draft dodgers. Yet fearing the growing unpopularity of the Vietnam War would damage Nixon's election, senior staff initiated a programme of illegal espionage against the Democratic Party. It would culminate in the most infamous political scandal in American history, ultimately destroying Nixon's presidency and his political reputation.

Since he was first elected to the White House in 1968, Richard Nixon had never shied away from attempts to undermine those he viewed as his enemies. In 1971, military analyst Daniel Ellsberg leaked what became known as the 'Pentagon Papers', illustrating how the scope of US military actions in Vietnam had been masked from the American public. In response, the so-called 'White House Plumbers' – a covert group created originally to prevent leaks of official papers – were instructed to break into the offices of Ellsberg's psychiatrist in an attempt to find material that might discredit him.

WATERGATE BREAK-IN

In January 1972 senior official G. Gordon Liddy held a presentation for fellow members of the Committee for the Re-election of the President (CRP). It recommended that covert and illegal activities should be considered to seek out campaign intelligence from the Democrats. Unknown to Nixon himself, a plan was approved that involved breaking into

the Democratic Party headquarters in Washington DC's Watergate complex to photograph official documents and install wiretapping devices inside telephones.

On the night of 28 May 1972, former CIA electronics expert James McCord and other ex-'plumbers' broke into the Watergate office building and made their way up to the sixth floor. Copies of top-secret documents were stolen and telephones used by two senior members of the Democratic Party's election campaign were bugged. The operation was only a partial success; the wiretaps were installed but failed to work properly. A second raid was organized for 17 June 1972. The plan swiftly unravelled when security guard Frank Wills spotted tape covering up door latches to create the impression that they were locked. Wills removed the tape but when he returned a short while later he discovered that it had been reapplied and called the police. When three plain clothes officers arrived on the scene at 2.30 a.m. they arrested former CIA electronics expert James McCord and four other burglars. In their possession were lock picks, cameras, rolls of unexposed film and a short-wave radio tuned to police frequencies.

President Nixon promised to turn over 1,200 pages of edited transcripts about the Watergate scandal to the House Judiciary Committee. That's the stack of transcripts in the background. He looked America in the eye and insisted they would clear him of any involvement.

THE GREAT COVER-UP

The Watergate break-in had not been authorized by Richard Nixon. His crime, though, was in colluding in its aftermath. The day following the arrests, Nixon and his chief of staff, H. R. Haldeman, discussed in private how the CIA might be used to block a formal FBI investigation. But the cover-up failed and the FBI were quickly able to establish connections between the burglars and the CRP. The first glimpse of a major scandal broke when an anonymous source known as 'Deep Throat' – only publicly identified 33 years later as deputy director of the FBI

Carl Bernstein and Bob Woodward, award-winning reporters on the Washington Post.

Mark Felt – leaked information to a pair of *Washington Post* investigative reporters, Bob Woodward and Carl Bernstein. It seemed that a $25,000 (£19,000) payment from Nixon's re-election campaign had been deposited into one of the burglar's bank accounts.

At this time, suspicions of a wider government conspiracy were viewed with scepticism or were simply not widely reported elsewhere. Nixon, however, went on the attack, proclaiming the *Post*'s coverage as politically motivated and misleading. At a news conference on 29 August 1972, President Nixon announced – untruthfully – that a full investigation had been launched by presidential counsel John Dean and that he could now state 'categorically' that 'no one in the White House staff, no one in this Administration, presently employed, was involved in this bizarre incident'.

'I'M NOT A CROOK'

When Richard Nixon was re-elected in November 1972 with an unprecedented landslide majority it seemed as if the Watergate affair would soon be forgotten. Yet within a matter of months the scandal would escalate to a point where Nixon's presidency would become untenable.

The Watergate burglars were convicted on 30 January 1973, but the FBI investigation was far from over. Soon four of Nixon's most senior White House aides found themselves facing prosecution for perjury and obstruction of justice. By the summer, the Watergate affair had snowballed and was now the subject of two official government investigations; one led by special prosecutor Archibald Cox, the other by North Carolina senator Sam Ervin. The most sensational revelation emerged in July, that Nixon had installed a secret taping system in the Oval Office, recording all of his phone calls and conversations. When Cox and Ervin demanded the release of the tapes the president refused, citing executive privilege, and he still refused to co-operate when they issued subpoenas. The White House suggested that written summaries of the taped conversations could be provided, but this was not deemed acceptable to special prosecutor Cox. Furious, Nixon responded by ordering his Attorney General, Elliot Richardson, to fire Cox but Richardson refused, resigning rather than carry out the order – as did his deputy, William Ruckelshaus. Nixon's Solicitor General, Robert Bork, was then made acting Attorney General. Controversially, he fired Cox and abolished the office of special prosecutor, a move that became known as the 'Saturday Night Massacre'.

Washington was outraged by such a display of arrogance and the clamour for Nixon to be impeached began to grow. Sensing that he was beginning to lose the trust of even his closest allies, on 17 November 1973 the president took part in an hour-long televised question and answer session with the press. It was here that a visibly tense Nixon infamously declared: 'In all of my years of public life I have never obstructed justice ... People have got to know whether or not their president is a crook. Well, I'm not a crook.'

He continued to maintain that he had never acted illegally, conceding only that he had 'made a mistake' in not supervising campaign activities more closely.

RESIGNATION

The year 1974 began with Nixon's State of the Union address, where he attempted to draw a line beneath the scandal, remarking that: 'One year of Watergate is enough.' But in March his former Attorney General, John Mitchell, former aides H. R. Haldeman and John Ehrlichman and four other former members of Nixon's staff were indicted for conspiracy, obstruction of justice and perjury. The grand jury had also wanted Nixon indicted but this was not deemed to be constitutionally possible for a sitting president.

In one last attempt to mollify the prosecution, the White House released 1,200 pages of carefully selected transcripts from the tapes. The content was still deemed insufficient, although the most conservative Republicans were shocked by the heavy and persistent use of profanities within the president's conversations. Finally, on 24 July, the Supreme Court unanimously voted that the tapes should be handed over. Nixon's fate was sealed by what became known as the 'Smoking Gun' tape. It revealed a conversation held on 23 June 1972 – one week after the arrests – in which Nixon and Haldeman could be heard discussing the payment made to one of the burglars and the intention to force the FBI to abandon its investigation.

Facing certain impeachment, on 8 August 1974 Richard Milhous Nixon announced his resignation live on television and radio. The following day, Vice President Gerald Ford was sworn into office.

CONTROVERSIAL PARDON

Although the Watergate affair was now over, there would be one final controversial postscript. Now Nixon had resigned there were many who wanted to see him punished. On 8 September 1974, President Ford granted Nixon a 'full, free and absolute pardon' for all crimes that he 'committed or may have committed'. The *New York Times* declared it a 'profoundly unwise, divisive and unjust act'. Gerald Ford would later agree that it was one of the major reasons behind his defeat to Jimmy Carter in the 1976 presidential election.

Richard Nixon at the White house. A few months later, he anounced his resignation as president on 9 August 1974.

The legacy of Watergate was profound and long-lasting. The affair brought terms such as 'cover-up' and 'leak' into the common vocabulary and even now any major scandal that hits the news headlines is liable to find itself suffixed with a '-gate'.

In the immediate aftermath, legislation was passed that sought to curb abuses of power within the CIA, the FBI and the country's other security agencies. Nevertheless, public confidence in elected office was shaken to the core. And it could be argued that it has never truly fully recovered.

Everything about the man polarizes opinion. Everything. There's no skirting around the fact that President Donald John Trump is the most controversial public figure of his generation. His supporters see him as the outsider who gatecrashed the Washington party, the man who understood the concerns of the nation's forgotten blue-collar workers, a saviour with a mission to 'Make America Great Again'. Others are less enamoured – comedian John Oliver described him as the 'man who will one day be remembered by his great-great-grandchildren as the reason they had to change their last names'.

SURPRISE PRESIDENT

Donald Trump first came to the attention of the public in 1971, when he was made chairman of his father's mighty real estate empire. Renaming it The Trump Organization, in 1978 he began a series of high-profile property developments in Manhattan, among them the 58-storey, 664-foot (202 m) skyscraper he named Trump Tower. He further engaged in high-profile side projects, such as ownership of the New Jersey Generals football team and the Miss Universe beauty pageants, not to mention his much-derided Trump University. Trump's fame spread beyond New York in 1987 with his international bestselling book *Trump: The Art of the Deal*, which helped establish his credentials as a businessman and entrepreneur. He was then quickly elevated to the position of television star, hosting the popular NBC reality show *The Apprentice*, and 12 years later he confounded detractors with his most unexpected career progression. With next to no experience of government politics, he secured the Republican Party nomination and was elected 45th president of the United States.

EX-WIFE'S ALLEGATION

The controversies surrounding Trump's domestic and foreign policies are already legion, as are his methods of hiring and firing White House staff, his expansive use of social media soundbites, his provocative remarks on race and gender ... and just about any other subject that catches his attention. Away from the subjective world of politics and business, however, throughout his adult life Donald Trump has faced persistent allegations relating to his attitudes and behaviour towards women. During that time, some very serious accusations have been raised.

The first story of alleged sexual abuse to reach the public came from his former wife, Ivana. Married in 1977, she filed for divorce in 1990 following his affair with actress Marla Maples. Interviewed for a biography about her ex-husband in 1993, she alleged that she had been a victim of a 'violent assault' and had confided in friends that she had been raped.

A few months later she began to backtrack: 'As a woman I felt violated ... I referred to this as a "rape" but I do not want my words to be interpreted in a literal or criminal sense.'

Donald Trump is probably the most controversial president of all time – either you love him or you loathe him.

Ivana Trump said she had been the victim of 'violent assault' by her husband, but later backtracked on her claim.

In 2015, when the incident came to light during the presidential campaign, Ivana Trump further played down its significance by saying that it came from 'a time of very high tension during my divorce'.

SELF-INCRIMINATION

A remarkable piece of self-incrimination surfaced shortly before Trump's crucial second presidential debate in 2016. The *Washington Post* published a video made in 2005 of an extraordinary conversation with *Access Hollywood* host Billy Bush. Trump described in detail his attempts to seduce presenter Nancy O'Dell and actor Arianne Zucker.

'You know, I'm automatically attracted to beautiful women – I just start kissing them. It's like a magnet. Just kiss. I don't even wait. And when you're a star, they let you do it. You can do anything. Grab 'em by the pussy. You can do anything!'

Trump's presidential opponent Hillary Clinton gave a swift response: 'This is horrific. We cannot allow this man to become president.' He also faced censure from many leading members of his own party – even his running mate, Mike Pence, was unimpressed: 'I do not condone his remarks and cannot defend them.'

As ever when faced with a bad press, Trump came out fighting. His first move was to write it off as 'locker room banter, a private conversation that took place many years ago'. Yet he couldn't resist a hurtful dig at his opponent: 'Bill Clinton has said far worse to me on the golf course – not even close.' Media commentators took the phrase 'grab 'em by the pussy' to mean touching a person's genitals without consent, which is patently sexual assault, and Trump did then show remorse for his ribald language.

'I'm not proud of it. I apologize to my family. I apologize to the American people.'

His third wife, Melania, also weighed into the debate. After describing his words as 'unacceptable and offensive', she said she hoped that America would 'accept his apology, as I have'. Trump would nevertheless always deny that he had ever assaulted a woman.

HUMAN OCTOPUS

The backlash ultimately had little impact on the election result, even if a PussyGrabsBack hashtag emerged imploring women not to vote for Trump, but it did encourage a number of other alleged victims to go public. Businesswoman Jessica Leeds told the *New York Times* that she had been assaulted on a passenger jet in the early 1980s; sitting alongside Trump in the first-class cabin, she claimed he had grabbed her breasts and tried to put his hand up her skirt.

'He was like an octopus ... his hands were everywhere.'

Trump called the story 'fiction' and threatened to sue if the allegations were not withdrawn. Although the *New York Times* refused to retract, no legal action was taken.

The first incident to result in a lawsuit being filed came in 1997 when Jill Harth, a former business partner, alleged that during a contract-signing celebration with her then boyfriend at Trump's Mar-a-Lago estate he had forcibly kissed her on the lips, groped her breasts and grabbed her genitals.

'He pushed me up against the wall ... and had his hands all over me.'

The lawsuit was later withdrawn.

By the beginning of 2019, sexual misconduct allegations had been made against Donald Trump by at least 19 women. Most related to unwanted physical contact, although a large number were reported by those appearing in Miss Universe franchises owned by Trump, including Miss USA and Miss Teen USA.

Melania Trump with her husband as they attend church on St Patrick's Day in Washington, 2019.

At a rally in October 2016 he referred to the women as 'horrible, horrible liars'.

But as Trump himself told shock jock Howard Stern: 'I'll go backstage before a show ... I'm allowed to go in because I'm the owner of the pageant ... You know, they're standing there with no clothes. And you see these incredible-looking women. And so I sort of get away with things like that.'

One of Trump's tactics in dealing with allegations has been to demean the accuser, in one case suggesting that he couldn't have sexually assaulted the woman because she was too unattractive. Journalist Natasha Stoynoff had alleged that he had 'forced his tongue down my throat', but he remarked with a smile: 'Look at her ... I don't think so.' (In January 2019, a play co-written by Stoynoff premiered in New York City, setting her experience to music and song!)

THE PRESIDENT AND THE PORN STAR

The most potentially damaging allegation emerged shortly before the 2016 presidential election. Rumours had begun to circulate that in 2006, just a few months after his third wife Melania had given birth to their son Barron, Trump had enjoyed a brief liaison with 27-year-old porn star Stephanie Clifford – better known to her fans as Stormy Daniels. Trump's lawyer, Michael Cohen, paid Daniels $130,000 (£100,000) hush money to suppress the story, the payment being subject to a non-disclosure agreement (NDA).

The scandal broke on 12 January 2018 when the *Wall Street Journal* reported the payment made by Cohen to the actress and questioned how it was funded. Cohen denied an affair had ever taken place but claimed to have made the payment out of his own pocket and without Trump's knowledge – a claim most found hard to believe. Daniels' lawyers, meanwhile, claimed that Cohen's admission voided the terms of the NDA, thereby freeing her to go public.

On 25 March 2018 Stormy Daniels was interviewed by Anderson Cooper for the CBS *60 Minutes* show. If her depiction of events was true, it would have both legal and political ramifications for the president. She began the interview by revealing that she had met Trump – 33 years her senior – at a celebrity golf tournament in Lake Tahoe and had been invited for a private dinner at his hotel suite. Trump had been dismissive when she asked him about his relationship with his wife – 'we don't

Adult film actress/director Stormy Daniels attends the 2019 Adult Video Awards in the Hard Rock Hotel, Las Vegas.

even … we have separate rooms and stuff'. Daniels claimed that she had spanked him with a rolled-up copy of *Forbes* magazine (with Trump on the cover, no less!), that they had sex on just one occasion and that the president had not used a condom. Trump, she maintained, had dangled the prize of a lucrative spot on his *Celebrity Apprentice* TV show, which he later withdrew.

HUSH MONEY

One day, while out with her infant daughter, she claimed to have been approached by a stranger with a terrifying message: 'Leave Trump alone. That's a beautiful little girl. It'd be a shame if something happened to her mom.' In October 2016, with Trump now a serious presidential candidate, Daniels was offered – and accepted – the $130,000 hush payment from Cohen.

After several weeks of media frenzy, during an investigation concerning a wide range of other issues, on 9 April 2018 FBI agents raided Michael Cohen's office, seizing emails and other business documents. Then on 2 May Rudy Giuliani, recently appointed as Trump's personal lawyer, went on record admitting that Trump 'did know the general arrangement' of the payments, and that Cohen had been repaid in full. Trump was then forced to admit that the payments were made in instalments, but maintained they were from his personal accounts and not, as was being widely reported, from presidential campaign funds.

> **Daniels claimed that she had spanked him with a rolled-up copy of *Forbes* magazine.**

On 21 August Michael Cohen was arrested by the FBI. He pleaded guilty to eight charges, including one count of 'making an excessive campaign contribution', which alluded to the hush money. Cohen implicated the president in his plea. Meanwhile, the *Wall Street Journal* reported that federal prosecutors now had evidence of Trump's 'central role' in the Stormy Daniels scandal, and described how the payments had violated campaign-finance law.

On 12 December 2018 Michael Cohen was sentenced to three years in prison, scheduled to begin on 6 May 2019. Following his sentence, he launched into his own public relations exercise, telling ABC News that Trump had been aware at the time that his actions were wrong but that he nevertheless 'directed me to make the payments'. Rudy Giuliani, meanwhile, downplayed the campaign violations: 'Nobody got killed, nobody got robbed. This was not a big crime.'

Even though it was not a part of his sentence, Cohen testified publicly before the House Committee on Oversight and Reform in January 2019, expressing remorse for things he had done on behalf of the president. Before a televised audience he variously described Trump as a 'con-man', a 'racist' and a 'cheat'.

In spite of Trump's continued denials, if it were to be proven that he had instructed Michael Cohen to break the law the legal ramifications could yet be hugely damaging to a presidency already shrouded in controversy.

CHAPPAQUIDDICK

Edward Moore Kennedy was raised in a family steeped in wealth, privilege and politics. His great-grandfather, Patrick Kennedy, had fled the Irish famine, arriving in Massachusetts in 1849. By the time 'Ted' was born in 1932, the family had amassed an impressive fortune, first as importers of Scotch whisky and later from investing in stocks and commodities. The Kennedy name was also a growing influence in the world of American politics.

GREAT EXPECTATIONS

Joseph P. Kennedy was a prominent member of the Democratic Party who had held a number of senior government positions before President Roosevelt appointed him the United States ambassador to the United Kingdom in 1938. And he had high hopes for his four sons.

The youngest of four brothers, Ted Kennedy had plenty of expectations to meet. His eldest brother, Joseph Patrick Jr., had been expected to run for congress in 1946 but was tragically killed in action at the end of the Second World War. It was John Fitzgerald – 'JFK' – who became the first Kennedy to achieve political power, first as a senator and then, of course, as the 35th president of the United States from 1961 until his assassination two years later.

Ted's other brother, Robert Francis ('Bobby'), was a high-profile lawyer who had guided JFK's presidential campaign before his own appointment as the 64th United States Attorney General; in 1968 he too was assassinated as he prepared his own presidential bid.

Like his brothers and father before him Ted Kennedy was educated at Harvard, but had not been a gifted student; at the end of his second semester he was expelled for cheating.

It was his family influence that later enabled him to be readmitted and he finally graduated in 1956. After his brother had become president, it was announced that, at the age of 30, Ted Kennedy would run for JFK's old office, that of senator for Massachusetts.

BOILER ROOM GIRLS

By 1969, Senator Edward Kennedy had established himself on Capitol Hill as a hard-working and diligent legislator with a strong social conscience. He was also an increasingly influential voice within the Democratic Party. Following the brutal assassination of his brother Bobby while on the campaign trail, it was assumed that Ted would soon be readying his own bid for America's highest office.

At the same time, gossip began circulating around Washington. The young senator was portrayed as a hard drinker with a voracious sexual appetite, who scarcely bothered to conceal his frequent affairs from his wife Joan.

In July 1969 Senator Kennedy headed back to Massachusetts to race his yacht at the Edgartown Regatta. On the evening of 18 July he hosted an intimate gathering at Lawrence Cottage on Chappaquiddick Island, an exclusive, secluded location accessible only by ferry from Martha's Vineyard. The party was held for the 'boiler room girls', a name given to a group of secretaries who had worked together on Bobby Kennedy's 1968 presidential campaign. Six young women were joined by the senator and five of his friends and colleagues, mostly middle-aged married men.

Portrait of the Kennedy family at Brookline, Massachusetts, in the 1930s. John F. Kennedy sits on the back of the sofa behind his father, Joseph Kennedy Sr., while youngest child Ted Kennedy, all in white, stands in the embrace of his dad.

FATEFUL DRIVE

According to Kennedy's testimony, at around 11.15 p.m. he announced that he was leaving the party. One of his guests, 28-year-old Mary Jo Kopechne, then asked if she could be dropped off at her hotel. Kennedy – who didn't usually drive – grabbed the keys from his chauffeur and set off in his Oldsmobile Delmont 88 for the ferry slip, where they would be able to take a boat back to Martha's Vineyard. While driving along the main drag Kennedy claimed to have taken a wrong turn on to an unpaved road, where he shot over the side of Dike Bridge, plunging into the tide-swept Poucha Pond below. The car was submerged and flipped on to its roof. Kennedy managed to break free of the vehicle and swim to safety but Kopechne was unable to escape. Local fire chief John Farrar later told the court that since the victim had suffocated in an air pocket rather than drowned, she would probably have survived if the police and rescue services had been alerted immediately.

Dike Bridge where Ted Kennedy's car left the road.

HE LEFT HER TO DIE

It was widely suspected that the local judiciary found itself under pressure from Massachusetts' most powerful family. That would certainly explain why Ted Kennedy escaped a potential charge of manslaughter, perjury and driving to endanger life and was charged only with leaving the scene of an accident. His testimony was sketchy and unconvincing, his actions showing more concern for his political career than for the life of a young woman. In court he claimed to have dived back into the water repeatedly after the accident but, unable to see his passenger, he had decided to walk the mile and a half back to Lawrence Cottage. His route would have taken him past four houses, the first of which was only 150 yards from Dike Bridge, but instead of waking the residents to call for help he had continued on his way. After informing his cousin Joe Gargan and friend Paul Markham, both also lawyers, he returned to the scene of the accident with them. Driving him to the ferry dock, where there was a public phone box, they implored Kennedy to call the police immediately but he ordered them back to the party, reportedly saying: 'You take care of the other girls; I will take care of the accident.' They assumed that he would make the call and left him to return to his hotel but Kennedy did not notify the police until the following morning, some ten hours later. In the meantime, he was later reported to have made 17 other calls.

A frogman attempts to raise the Oldsmobile Delmont 88 driven by Kennedy eight hours after it plunged into the water.

SCANDAL SHOCKS AMERICA

A week later, Senator Kennedy pleaded guilty to leaving the scene of an accident and was given a two-month suspended jail sentence. That evening he gave a lengthy prepared statement that was broadcast live by the television networks. He denied the suspicions of 'immoral conduct' or that he had been 'driving under the influence of liquor'. Instead, he claimed that he had suffered 'cerebral concussion and shock' after the accident and had been overcome by 'all kinds of scrambled thoughts ... by a jumble of emotions ... grief, fear, doubt, exhaustion, panic, confusion, and shock'.

The scandal shocked America. By Kennedy's own admission, his actions had been 'irrational and indefensible and inexcusable and inexplicable'. The most commonly held view remains that Kennedy had been drinking heavily and had panicked after the accident, afraid of the damaging publicity a police report would cause. (Reporters at the scene noted a large trash

can filled with beer cans and liquor bottles being removed from the cottage.) Many also found it hard to believe his claims that there was 'no impropriety' at the party or that no 'immoral conduct' had taken place between himself and Mary Jo Kopechne. Kennedy would nevertheless continue to maintain that his testimony was the truth.

Edward Kennedy (in a neck brace) and his wife Joan return from the funeral of Mary Jo Kopechne, 22 July 1969.

END OF PRESIDENTIAL HOPES

Even though he only received a suspended sentence, Chappaquiddick effectively ended Ted Kennedy's chances of ever becoming president. With media interest in the scandal still rife, he pledged not to run in 1972 and 1976 and he finally lost out to Jimmy Carter for the 1980 Democratic nomination. Carter alluded to the incident several times during head-to-head TV debates, declaring that he himself had never 'panicked in a crisis'.

Ted Kennedy was never fully able to escape the spectre of the Chappaquiddick tragedy. He would continue to serve as senator for Massachusetts right up until his death in 2009 at the age of 77 and left behind him a much-admired political reputation as one of the great legislators in American politics. His posthumous memoir, *True Compass*, showed his remorse. He denied there had ever been any romantic involvement with Mary Jo Kopechne, but admitted nonetheless: 'That night on Chappaquiddick Island ended in a horrible tragedy that haunts me every day of my life.'

THE PEOPLE'S PRINCESS

Towards the end of her life, Diana, Princess of Wales, by her own admission, had become a 'nuisance' to the British establishment. Now, all of a sudden, she was gone, killed in a car crash in Paris. For conspiracy theorists everywhere, that was simply too convenient.

DEATH OF A PRINCESS

On the morning of Sunday, 31 August 1997 the world awoke to the most shocking news headlines. Shortly after midnight, Diana, Princess of Wales, had been involved in a road accident in Paris. The 36-year-old princess was rushed to hospital but never regained consciousness. Her driver had lost control of the black Mercedes S280 in which she was travelling as it sped through the Alma tunnel alongside the river Seine while being pursued by photographers on motorcycles. Also killed in the crash was her partner, Dodi Fayed, heir to billionaire Egyptian businessman Mohamed Al-Fayed. In Britain, Diana's death saw an unprecedented outpouring of public grief. More than 2.5 billion people worldwide watched her funeral on television, and Elton John's tribute, 'Candle in the Wind 1997', became the biggest-selling single since the creation of the pop music charts in the 1950s.

FAIRYTALE TURNS SOUR

Lady Diana Spencer first made the news in 1980, when rumours began circulating that she was the new love interest of Prince Charles, heir to the British throne. When Buckingham Palace announced their engagement in February 1981, wedding fever struck the nation. The biggest day in the royal calendar since the coronation of Queen Elizabeth II almost 30 years earlier, the royal wedding on 29 July 1981 was declared a public holiday – it would be a day of street parties and national celebration. Adored by the public, overnight the shy, 20-year-old Princess of Wales became a permanent feature on the front pages of newspapers and fashion magazines, her every move pursued relentlessly by the paparazzi. Celebrations were sounded once again when four months later it was announced that Diana was pregnant: on 21 June 1982 she gave birth to the couple's first son, Prince William, third in line to the throne. A second son, Prince Harry, followed two years later.

Yet what the world saw as a fairytale wedding quickly soured into a deeply unhappy marriage. Divided by a 13-year age gap, Charles and Diana seemed to have very little in common. A serious and studious man, Charles was steeped in the rituals of royalty and its traditional rural pursuits. Diana, on the other hand, was young, playful and by her own reckoning 'as thick as a plank'. And she struggled with the demands of her official duties. Diana's unhappiness led to a deterioration in her health. She first developed the eating disorder bulimia, but there were other issues she had to face. During her first pregnancy she was badly bruised after falling down a staircase at Sandringham; shockingly, she would later claim that it had been a deliberate act.

'I was about to cut my wrists,' she would recall. 'I was in such a bad way. Couldn't sleep, didn't eat, the whole world was collapsing around me. All the analysts and psychiatrists you can ever dream of came plodding in.'

CAMILLAGATE

Although Charles and Diana successfully stage-managed their public duties together, behind the scenes the marriage was unravelling. Charles had rekindled his relationship with old flame Camilla Parker Bowles. ('Well, there were three of us in this marriage, so it was a bit crowded,' Diana told the BBC in 1995.) The affair was exposed in 1992, following the publication of *Diana: Her True Story*, by Andrew Morton, and again in January 1993, a month after the official split between the Prince and Princess of Wales, when a 1989 recording of a sexually explicit conversation between Prince Charles and Camilla Parker Bowles, dubbed the Camillagate tape, was transcribed and published by the press.

Lady Diana Spencer married Prince Charles in 1981; they divorced in 1996 after well-publicized extramarital affairs by both parties.

DIANA'S AFFAIRS

The princess would also engage in a number of well-documented relationships. While suffering post-natal depression in 1984, she was alleged to have begun an affair with her bodyguard, Barry Mannakee. Swiftly dispatched from his post, nine months later Mannakee was killed in a motorcycle accident. Diana remained convinced that he had been murdered by the British secret service. Her most famous liaison, though, was with cavalry officer Major James Hewitt. The affair lasted five years, Diana later admitting in an interview: 'Yes, I adored him. Yes, I loved him.' In spite of his own denials, rumours still persist that Hewitt is the biological father of Prince Harry, but other sources maintain that Diana did not meet Hewitt until two years after his birth.

CCTV footage showing Dodi Fayed buying an engagement ring in Paris for Diana hours before they were both killed in the car crash.

There were also the pre-1990 'Squidgygate' tapes. Revealed by the *Sun* in 1992, they provided a record of intimate conversations between Diana and James Gilbey, an alleged lover. Gilbey called the princess 'Squidgy' in the conversations and often referred to her as 'darling'. At one point she mentioned her concern about being pregnant. Some of Diana's friends were of the opinion that the tapes were leaked to smear her reputation at a crucial time in the royal couple's relationship. At a 2008 inquest into the princess's death, her former bodyguard, Ken Wharfe, said he believed that the tapes were recorded by the British intelligence listening station GCHQ.

SEPARATION

In December 1992, after years of speculation and negative media stories, it came as no surprise when Prime Minister John Major announced Charles and Diana's 'amicable separation' to the House of Commons. Both Charles and Diana would take part in carefully choreographed 'tell-all' public relations interviews with British television, the tiniest aspects of their lives ever under scrutiny. Their divorce was finalized on 28 August 1996. Despite hostility in some quarters of the English press, Diana continued to be hugely popular, using her celebrity to influence projects that she held close, such as HIV/AIDS charities and the banning of landmines. Prince Charles would later marry Camilla Parker Bowles.

CONSPIRACY THEORIES

If well-publicized marital infidelity among principal members of the royal family were not scandalous enough, what are we to make, then, of the conspiracy claims that abounded following Diana's death? The idea first came from Diana herself. In October 1993 she wrote a letter to her butler, Paul Burrell, claiming that Charles had been having an affair with his PA, Tiggy Legge-Bourke, and that there were plans for 'an "accident" in my car, brake failure and serious head injury in order to make the path clear for Charles to marry'. After all, her bodyguard had died in an accident that she believed had been planned. Whatever the truth, Diana had long believed that the establishment were out to 'get her'.

Another popular theory was that Henri Paul, the driver of the car, who also perished in the accident, was in the pay of unspecified security services and had been ordered to cause the crash intentionally. Paul was widely held as a scapegoat by the tabloid press. Having undergone treatment for alcoholism, blood tests did show alcohol in his system, although there was no suggestion that he was drunk at the wheel.

Mohamed Al-Fayed, owner of Harrods and the father of Dodi Fayed, had his own theory. He believed that Diana was pregnant and that the royal family 'could not accept that an Egyptian Muslim could eventually be the stepfather of the future king of England'. In his view, MI6 had been instructed to carry out the murder. Diana and Dodi Fayed had been holidaying together in France before the accident and there had been some newspaper speculation that she might be pregnant. The post-mortem nonetheless showed no such signs. Fayed remained unconvinced, making the surprising claim that Prince Philip, the Duke of Edinburgh, had been behind the plot.

Tabloid speculation and Mr Fayed's persistence would eventually create pressure for an official inquiry. The Metropolitan Police launched Operation Paget in 2004 to investigate more than 50 separate conspiracy claims. Two years later, at a cost of almost £4 million ($5.2m), the 832-page criminal investigation report was published.

Its conclusions were hardly dramatic: 'There was no conspiracy to murder any of the occupants of the car. This was a tragic accident ... there was no cover-up.'

The subsequent coroner's inquest concluded that Diana and Dodi Fayed had been 'unlawfully killed' as a result of the 'speed and manner of driving of the Mercedes' and the 'impairment of the judgement of the driver of the Mercedes through alcohol'. It also cited the pursuing paparazzi and the lack of seatbelt use as contributing factors.

A tragic accident? That remains the official verdict. But more than two decades on, the speculation continues. The grieving father, Mohammed Al-Fayed, would remain bitterly unconvinced. This was a grand cover-up by the royal family and the British establishment, he maintained. 'I will not rest,' he declared, 'until I expose the devastation and loss these gangsters have inflicted on me.'

A tragic accident? That remains the official verdict.

Prince Philip, Prince William, 9th Earl Charles Spencer (Diana's brother), Prince Harry and Prince Charles walk behind the funeral cortege, 6 September 1997.

THE PROFUMO AFFAIR

Even as the 1960s dawned, the United Kingdom continued to display the last vestiges of post-war torpor. Food rationing remained fresh in people's minds and many of its major towns and cities still bore visible signs of Luftwaffe air raids. Conservative and class-conscious, at its heart was an age-old reverence for the aristocracy and politicians. But that was all about to change.

SOCIAL REVOLUTION

Britain was on the cusp of a social revolution as it witnessed the early days of a new liberal society that would usher in the Swinging Sixties. The relationship between media and government was also changing. The deference once shown to the ruling elite – an unwritten agreement that Parliament and royalty should never have to face embarrassment – was severely tested in 1962 when two reporters were controversially jailed for refusing to name their sources during a Cold War espionage scandal. While the intention may have been to curb reporting on sensitive matters, some newspaper editors were angered, seeing it as a challenge to press freedom. As the *New Statesman* magazine commented at the time, anyone in government found to be involved in a scandal would now have to expect 'the full treatment'.

KEELER, WARD AND THE RUSSIAN ATTACHÉ

John Dennis Profumo had the most impeccable of credentials. Educated at Harrow and Oxford, his political career had elevated him to the position of Secretary of State for War in the Conservative government of Harold Macmillan.

He was also married to film actress Valerie Hobson and was a well-known figure within London's glamorous social circles. In 1961, however, gossip and rumour had begun circulating over his private life, in particular his relationship with 20-year-old model Christine Keeler.

After an unhappy childhood Keeler had left her Berkshire home at the age of 16, soon finding work as a topless dancer at Murray's, a Soho cabaret club. It was here that she met society osteopath Stephen Ward and soon afterwards she moved into his Wimpole Mews house. Keeler and her fellow 'hostess', Mandy Rice-Davies, were introduced to many of Ward's society friends, among them politician Lord Astor, famed for the lavish soirées thrown at Cliveden, his grand Buckinghamshire estate. Ward loved the aristocracy as much as he loved young women and he delighted in mixing together the high life with the low.

He was also an accomplished artist, supplementing the already considerable income from his practice by sketching pictures of his wealthy and famous social connections. Ward had wanted to visit Russia to draw portraits of some of the Soviet leaders and through one of his patients he was able to meet Captain Yevgeny Ivanov, a naval attaché at the Soviet Embassy. At the height of the Cold War tensions MI5 considered Ivanov, with his apparent fondness for life in the West, as a potential defector and approached Ward for assistance. Ward and Ivanov soon became good friends, often spending time at Wimpole Mews with Keeler and Rice-Davies: MI5, it was claimed, had planned to use the attractive Keeler in a honeytrap operation to secure Ivanov's defection.

Mandy Rice-Davies (left) and Christine Keeler are driven away from the Old Bailey after the first day of the Stephen Ward trial.

PROFUMO MEETS KEELER

On 8 July 1961, Ward, Ivanov and Keeler attended one of Lord Astor's gatherings at Cliveden. As she was drying herself down after a naked swim in the outdoor pool, Keeler was introduced to one of Astor's guests, John Profumo. She had no idea who Profumo was at this time, but had been impressed by the fact that he was married to a film star. Smitten with the young 'freelance model', Profumo promised he would be in contact with her. As the weekend drew to a close Ward asked Keeler to take Ivanov back to Wimpole Mews where, she would later claim, they slept together. Reporting the events to MI5, Ward maintained that Ivanov had been asking him questions about planned nuclear arms deployment in West Germany.

Back in London, Profumo and Christine Keeler began their infamous, if brief, affair, usually rendezvousing at Ward's house. Keeler claimed that during this time Stephen Ward had asked her to procure information about nuclear weapons from Profumo but that she had not done so.

John Profumo, Britain's former minister of war, drives his car home with his actress wife, Valerie Hobson, alongside him. He had resigned his post after admitting an affair with Christine Keeler.

On 11 August 1961, Cabinet Secretary Sir Norman Brook informally interviewed Profumo, advising him to give a wide berth to Ward and his social circle. His message was clear: MI5 now had severe reservations about Stephen Ward and knew about his relationship with Christine Keeler. Profumo ended the affair that same day, but rumours of a love triangle between an unspecified government minister, a Soviet diplomat and a 'call girl' nevertheless began to seep into magazine gossip columns. The Soviet government took no chances and Captain Ivanov was recalled to Moscow.

LIES TO PARLIAMENT

Drama surrounded Christine Keeler at the end of 1962. On 14 December one of her rejected lovers, Johnny Edgecombe, was arrested for firing pistol shots outside Wimpole Mews after she'd refused to see him and the subsequent trial saw Christine Keeler's name in the newspapers for the first time. Increasingly indiscreet, Keeler met a former MP named John Lewis in a nightclub and told him the whole story, unaware that Lewis held a long-standing personal grudge against Ward. Lewis then reported Ward to the police as a national security risk and for living off immoral earnings. He also passed the information to his friend, MP George Wigg, who sparked controversy by asking questions in the House of Commons about rumours linking 'a minister' to Keeler, Ivanov and the Edgecombe shooting incident. Everyone in Parliament knew that the unnamed man was John Profumo and he was advised to issue an immediate rebuttal. He agreed that he had met Captain Ivanov twice and claimed there had been 'no impropriety in my acquaintanceship with Miss Keeler'.

HUGE EMBARRASSMENT

Knowing John Profumo had lied to Parliament, the press went ahead and published the full story. Profumo could no longer remain in government and on 5 June 1963 he confessed to having 'misled' Parliament. He resigned from office immediately. Most commentators agreed that his fate was sealed the moment he lied to the House of Commons. Profumo would never speak publicly of the scandal that ended his career. No breach of national security was known to have resulted from the affair, but it was a huge embarrassment to the government and a factor in the Conservative Party's defeat in the 1964 general election.

WARD'S SUICIDE

Stephen Ward, meanwhile, was charged with living off the 'immoral earnings' of Keeler, Rice-Davies and two other prostitutes. Much of the evidence was circumstantial and while the prosecution seemed to have a weak case it was delivered with a ferocity that shocked Ward. On 31 July 1963, following judge Sir Archie Marshall's hostile summing-up, Stephen Ward returned to his house where he took an overdose of barbiturates. He died three days later.

The Profumo affair had it all – sex, lies, espionage, a middle-aged politician brought down by his infatuation with a pretty young woman and a fall-guy who would pay with his life. It became one of the most famous of all British scandals and a part of the nation's popular culture. Britain had never seen anything like the Profumo affair and it remains the sex scandal against which all others are still measured.

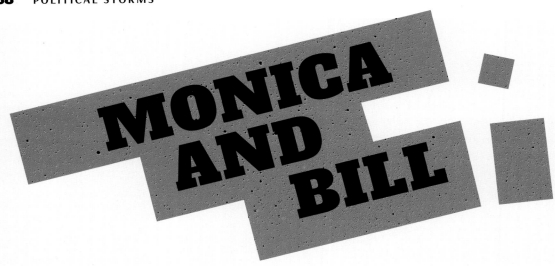

MONICA AND BILL

Sex and politics. It was an irresistible combination that came together spectacularly at the start of 1998 when the Drudge Report, then a little-known right-wing political news website, broke the story of a suspected affair between William Jefferson Clinton, 42nd president of the United States, and a young White House intern named Monica Lewinsky.

SKELETONS IN THE CLOSET

Popular and charismatic, Bill Clinton had been elected to the Oval Office in 1992, but his 17-year marriage to lawyer Hillary Rodham Clinton was already known to be a complex one. Even as governor of Arkansas, Bill Clinton's marital infidelities had threatened to derail his political ambitions. Some close to him suggested that there were so many skeletons lurking that he ought to reconsider running for president, but here was a man who found the temptations of high office hard to resist. One of his pre-presidential conquests, Marla Crider, would remark that, even then, 'it was like flies to honey'; that women were 'literally mesmerised' by him.

OVAL OFFICE MEETINGS

Twenty-one-year-old Monica Lewinsky had just graduated with a degree in psychology when in July 1995 a family connection led to an unpaid internship at the White House. Lewinsky immediately caught the eye of the 48-year-old president, and by November they'd begun to meet covertly in the Oval Office. The salacious details of the affair would later spark a national debate as to what precisely constituted a sexual relationship. According to Lewinsky's own account, she and Clinton enjoyed nine 'encounters', all of which took place in the Oval Office between November 1995 and March 1997. None of them, she claimed, involved sexual intercourse. Instead they were mainly fellatio, in most cases without reaching ejaculation. (The most sensational tale described how

Clinton once penetrated Lewinsky with a cigar, which he then placed back in his mouth, telling her: 'It tastes good!')

In 1996, as suspicious senior White House staff began noticing Lewinsky's frequent presence around the Oval Office, she found herself transferred to the Office of Public Affairs at the Pentagon. According to Lewinsky, Clinton terminated their affair on 24 May 1997, two months after their final encounter. At that moment, he allegedly confided that he'd had 'hundreds' of extra-marital affairs but since turning 40 he had tried to be faithful to his wife. Lewinsky made several attempts to revive the relationship but Clinton remained resolute.

LEWINSKY CONFIDES IN COLLEAGUE

Most of Bill Clinton's alleged affairs were never made public. Monica Lewinsky, however, had been discussing her love life with a colleague. The consequences for everyone involved would be disastrous. Although Linda Tripp was more than two decades her senior, the Pentagon co-workers had become close confidantes. Unknown to Lewinsky, however, Tripp – at the suggestion of literary agent Lucianne Goldberg – had begun covertly recording their intimate late-night phone calls and would tape more than 20 hours of private conversation. In what would later be a headline story in its own right, Tripp also convinced Lewinsky not to dry-clean a blue dress that had been marked with a semen stain while she had been with Clinton.

Bill Clinton paused for thought when asked about Monica Lewinsky, former White House intern. Then he softened and said he hoped Lewinsky would have a good life and could get help if she needed it to get over the trauma of the scandal.

EARLIER HARASSMENT CASE

Clinton had already been named in a sexual harassment case in 1994. A woman named Paula Jones alleged that three years earlier, while he was still governor of Arkansas, Clinton had propositioned her in a hotel and had exposed himself to her. The ensuing case dragged on until 1998 and had important legal ramifications; namely that a sitting president could not – as Clinton's attorney had attempted – claim immunity from civil law litigation. Equally significant, though, was the fact that when Monica Lewinsky was called as a witness by Paula Jones's lawyers, who were attempting to establish a pattern of inappropriate behaviour by Clinton, she swore an affidavit denying any sexual relationship between her and the president. It was also claimed that Lewinsky had urged Linda Tripp to commit perjury to conceal the relationship.

DENIES AFFAIR

Clinton was already being officially investigated at this time by Independent Counsel Kenneth W. Starr. Appointed in 1994, Starr's original remit was to look into the failed Whitewater property deal in which the Clintons were implicated, but the investigation took a new direction when Starr was approached by Linda Tripp, who agreed to hand over the Lewinsky tapes.

By the end of 1997, Lucianne Goldberg had begun making approaches to the press. It was on 17 January 1998 that the Drudge Report website broke its story that *Newsweek* magazine was sitting on the most explosive White House scandal since the Iran–Contra affair. Four days later the story appeared in the *Washington Post*. Clinton fought back immediately and called a press conference where – wife Hillary solemnly at his side – he infamously remarked: 'I did not have sexual relations with that woman, Miss Lewinsky ... these allegations are false.'

STARR REPORT

Now certain that the president had committed perjury, Kenneth Starr offered Monica Lewinsky immunity from prosecution for having lied in the Paula Jones case on condition that she testified about her true relationship with President Clinton. She also agreed to turn over her blue dress; DNA testing subsequently showed the semen stain to have come from Clinton. In his grand jury video testimony, Clinton was forced to admit that his relationship with Lewinsky was 'inappropriate', although he still argued that since vaginal intercourse had never taken place with Monica Lewinsky he did not view it as a sexual relationship.

The 445-page 'Starr Report' was delivered on 9 September 1998. Two days later Congress voted 363–63 that the document should be made public. It was estimated that when it went online it was browsed by more than 20 million people – 12 per cent of adult Americans. On 21 September, Clinton's grand jury testimony was broadcast on national television. The Starr Report was

'I did not have sexual relations with that woman, Miss Lewinsky ...'

BILL CLINTON

A photograph showing Clinton standing next to Lewinsky at a White House function, 21 September 1998. Everybody's smiling...

controversial, its methods were questioned and it was widely viewed as being politically charged and partisan. Clinton himself described the investigation as a 'witch hunt'. Nevertheless, a vote for impeachment proceedings to begin was passed a month later. But Clinton still refused to resign.

IMPEACHMENT

The first US president since Andrew Johnson in 1869 to be impeached, Clinton was accused of perjury and the obstruction of justice. At the end of a 21-day trial, on 12 February 1999 the Senate voted 55 to 45 that Clinton was not guilty of perjury and 50–50 on the obstruction charge. Since a two-thirds majority was required on both counts, Clinton was officially acquitted.

Let's not forget that while Bill Clinton's political reputation was severely damaged, Monica Lewinsky's world was torn apart. Publicly shamed by America's media (comedian Jay Leno referred to her as 'The Slut in the Hat'), she found it impossible to resume a normal life. In March 2019 she still recalled the 'avalanche of pain and humiliation' that she faced on a daily basis. In recent years she has re-emerged as an activist with a sharp, witty presence on social media.

In spite of the controversies, Bill Clinton's presidency is still widely regarded as one of the most successful of the past century. Even throughout the Lewinsky scandal, Clinton's popularity remained high, with less than a third of Americans believing that he ought to have faced impeachment proceedings at all. By the time he left office in 2001 his personal approval figure was still 65 per cent – much the highest of any exiting president – although that inevitably fell when questions as to his honesty and morality were asked. In musing on his exit ratings, it was perhaps ABC News that most neatly characterized the Clinton era: 'You can't trust him, he's got weak morals and ethics – and he's done a heck of a good job.'

THE MAN THEY COULDN'T BRING DOWN

Known among his countrymen as *Il Cavaliere* ('The Knight'), for three decades Italian media mogul Silvio Berlusconi has been at the very centre of Italian political life, enjoying nine controversial years as prime minister – the longest period served in office by any individual since Benito Mussolini. During that time, convictions for tax fraud, allegations of corruption, inflammatory public remarks – not to mention the numerous sex scandals – ensured that Berlusconi's name would never be too far away from the headlines. Yet somehow he has managed to retain a large core of popular support, his political life – even in his ninth decade – still far from over.

BIRTH OF A BUSINESSMAN

Born in Milan in 1936, Silvio Berlusconi studied law at university and first made his mark in business as a property speculator, soon moving into the developing new world of cable television. He founded Fininvest in 1987, a holding company that would soon include Mediaset, Italy's largest commercial broadcaster, TV channel Canale 5 and the famous AC Milan football team.

ENTERS POLITICS

In the early 1990s, with corruption rife within Italian politics and business, the so-called *mani pulite* ('clean hands') investigations uncovered criminal activity on an unprecedented scale. Thousands of public figures came under suspicion and bribes paid by Italian and foreign companies bidding for major government contracts were estimated to have been worth approaching $4 billion (£3.1bn). The investigations and convictions created chaos within the political system, many of Italy's traditional parties being dissolved or torn apart. It was in this environment that Silvio Berlusconi announced his entry into politics with the formation of Forza Italia ('Forward Italy').

The new centre-right party won its first general election in March 1994, with leader Berlusconi becoming prime minister in a coalition government with the Lega Nord ('Northern League'). Hailed by his supporters as a reforming political outsider, it was nonetheless widely supposed that Berlusconi's dramatic appearance at the forefront of Italian politics was motivated more by a desire to shield himself and his businesses from

mani pulite scrutiny. As it happened, Berlusconi was forced to resign only eight months into his first period in office, when his coalition partners pulled out after discovering that he was being investigated for bribery.

Silvio Berlusconi made up and ready for the TV cameras; Il Cavaliere has lived much of his life in the fierce glare of publicity.

CONVICTED OF FRAUD

The first of Berlusconi's many legal scrapes took place in 1998, when he was convicted of bribing tax inspectors and accountancy fraud. He received a 33-month sentence but, as would so often be the case, the conviction was later overturned on appeal.

Berlusconi ran for government again in 2001, this time as leader of the right-wing coalition La Casa delle Libertà ('House of Freedoms'). Once again he was elected prime minister. His second premiership lasted for five years and would be characterized by controversial legislation that critics, such as his successor Romano Prodi, regarded as *ad personam* – that is, created to benefit his own legal and business problems. In 2002, his government passed laws to shorten statutory terms for tax fraud, enabling him to avoid conviction through being 'timed out' by the new statute of limitations. He would use the same procedure to overturn five other trials.

DIVORCE

The headlines that grabbed most attention, though, were unconnected with Berlusconi's legal obfuscation. In 2006, a former showgirl turned politician, Mara Carfagna, won a seat in parliament representing Forza Italia. On her first day in office, Berlusconi joked that his party practised *jus primae noctis* – a medieval right of a feudal lord to take the virginity of a young woman!

A year later, on stage at a television award show, Berlusconi remarked to Carfagna: 'If I wasn't already married I would have married you immediately ... with you I'd go anywhere.' His wife, former actress Veronica Lario, was outraged and, through a national newspaper, demanded an apology.

'I beg you, forgive me,' her husband proclaimed, 'and accept this public display of a private pride that gives in to your rage as an act of love.' But shortly afterwards he was in trouble again, this time when celebrity magazine *Oggi* published photographs of him holding hands with young women at his Sardinian retreat.

Berlusconi made an art form of brushing off scandal. Even after *Chi* magazine reported that prostitutes had been paid to attend parties at his residence, in May 2008 he nonetheless won a third term as Italy's prime minister. The Berlusconis' marital soap opera continued to enthral Italy, but a year later Veronica Lario's patience was finally spent. Having

Funtime girl Nadia Macri (centre), allegedly an acquaintance of Berlusconi, appears as 'special guest' at a bunga-bunga party at the Sopravento Disco Club in Rosignano Marittimo, 2011.

been photographed attending an 18th birthday gathering for aspiring model and TV actress Noemi Letizia, Berlusconi was served his divorce papers. Lario claimed dismissively that her husband 'consorts with minors'.

PAID FOR SEX WITH A MINOR

In spite of the gossip and rumours, it wasn't until 2011 that Silvio Berlusconi's infamous adventuring – 'it's better to be fond of beautiful women than to be gay' – involved the law courts. It was a case that combined sex with corruption and would captivate Italy for several years. On 27 May 2010, a 17-year-old Moroccan prostitute and belly dancer named Karima El Mahroug was arrested in Milan, accused of the theft of €3,000 (£2,600/$3,340). El Mahroug, known professionally as Ruby Rubacuori ('Ruby the Heartstealer'), contacted Berlusconi and after he had made repeated calls to senior police officials she was released. When the story reached the media, Berlusconi found himself under investigation for allegedly having sex with the underage prostitute and for abusing his office in procuring her release.

At the same time, a connected story was reported about 'a vast pimping network' providing underage prostitutes for Berlusconi's so-called 'bunga-bunga' parties. As was often the case, he denied all charges and allegations with a quip: 'I'm 74 years old and even though I may be a bit of a rascal, 33 girls in two months seems to me too much even for a 30-year-old.' Nevertheless, a month later he was officially charged with paying for sex with a minor (neither sex with a person between 14 and 17 nor adult prostitution is illegal in Italy, but *paying* for sex with a person under 18 is a crime) and the more serious offence of '*concussione*' – abuse of his public office.

BUNGA-BUNGA TRIAL

After two years of adjournments, and 50 court hearings, the trial – known in the press as the 'bunga-bunga trial' or 'Rubygate' – was concluded on 24 June 2013. Berlusconi was found guilty of both charges, sentenced to prison for seven years and banned from public office for life. This would, of course, be far from the end of the story. An appeal was swiftly lodged and in July 2014 his conviction was dramatically overturned, the presiding judge reaching the surprise conclusion that his actions 'did not constitute a crime'. After the acquittal was upheld by the high court in March 2015, 78-year-old Berlusconi declared that the decision 'has lifted a burden from my heart'. He vowed to make yet another return to the chaotic world of Italian politics.

The 'bunga-bunga' story took another bizarre twist on 1 March 2019 when 33-year-old Imane Fadil, a Moroccan model who testified against Berlusconi in 2012, died in a Milan hospital. Italian media suggest that she might have been poisoned with a radioactive substance. A regular guest at Berlusconi's sex parties, Fadil was writing a book about her experiences.

Berlusconi's legal history is a deeply complex one. He has been at the centre of numerous court actions, many of which would run concurrently. Many are still to reach a conclusion or are subject to appeals. Yet whatever the result, history suggests that the irrepressible Berlusconi will be as unlikely as ever to face any severe punishment.

EDWARD AND MRS SIMPSON

When King George V died on 20 January 1936, his eldest son Edward ascended the throne of Great Britain. His relationship with Wallis Simpson, a married American socialite, had already caused two years of consternation within the royal household. But in spite of his father's disapproval it was clear that Edward viewed Mrs Simpson as much more than a brief flirtation.

THE PLAYBOY PRINCE

It was well known that King George had long despaired of Edward's reckless womanizing and his inability to settle, remarking – presciently – that his second son, Albert, would be far better suited to the throne. He had already outraged the king by breaking with custom and introducing Wallis Simpson to his mother at a formal Buckingham Palace gathering. The British press regarded her as an ambitious social climber, but deference to the royal family resulted in only limited domestic media coverage. Stories of the 'playboy prince' and his American mistress were nonetheless widely reported abroad.

ABDICATION

Following the death of King George V, Edward made clear his intention to marry Mrs Simpson, creating a potential constitutional crisis. As head of the Church of England, a reigning monarch was unable to marry a divorcee – and Wallis Simpson would be twice divorced by the time she married Edward.

With preparations for the new monarch's May 1937 coronation under way, it became impossible to keep the sensational story from the public. As the scandal broke, Wallis Simpson fled to the south of France. It was made abundantly clear to the king that the

British government viewed her as unsuitable for the role of his consort, so Edward was left with little room for manoeuvre: if he were to marry Mrs Simpson he would have to renounce the throne.

On 11 December 1936, King Edward VIII broadcast his intention to abdicate: 'I have found it impossible to carry the heavy burden of responsibility, and to discharge my duties as king as I would wish to do, without the help and support of the woman I love.'

MARRIAGE AND EXILE

It was the most dramatic moment for the British monarchy since the Restoration. The throne passed to Edward's younger brother, Albert, Duke of York, who became King George VI. Edward was given the title of Duke of Windsor and a year later, following her divorce, he married Wallis Simpson. Ever mindful of protocol, King George VI forbade members of the royal family from attending the ceremony: like many Britons, he considered Edward's abdication an unforgivable dereliction of his birthright.

After they were married they were cast out by the British establishment, so the Duke and Duchess of Windsor left Britain and settled in France. The years that followed have since been the subject of endless controversy and speculation, with claims in some circles that the Duke of Windsor betrayed his country during wartime.

NAZI LINKS

Edward would first upset the British government in October 1937 when against official advice he and his wife visited Nazi Germany, where they were hosted by Adolf Hitler at his Bavarian retreat. The Duke and Duchess of Windsor relished the regal treatment they were given – it was in stark contrast to their *personae non gratae* status in the UK. Whether Edward actually was a Nazi sympathizer is open to debate, but the US press in 1940 reported his admiration for the way in which Hitler had reformed Germany.

The first portrait of the Duke and Duchess of Windsor after their marriage at the Chateau de Cande in Monts, France, June 1937. The wedding took place about six months after Edward gave up the throne.

The FBI went as far as informing the British government that they believed the Duchess of Windsor had been a Nazi spy.

Many of the official papers detailing concerns or allegations against Edward were unreleased to the public for decades. One of the claims was that he had leaked Allied war plans for the defence of Belgium and had advised Hitler to continue the Nazi air raids on London as a way of forcing a peace settlement. There is scant documentary evidence to support such allegations. What is certain is that the US government was sufficiently troubled by the Windsors that they were kept under surveillance during a visit in 1940. The FBI went as far as informing the British government that they believed the Duchess of Windsor had been a Nazi spy. In a secret memo, they alleged that she had been passing secrets to Germany's foreign minister, Joachim von Ribbentrop, and that they had been former lovers.

Much of what we know about the Duke of Windsor's attitude towards Nazi Germany comes from a set of documents known as the Marburg Files. Discovered by American troops at the end of the war in 1945, these were official Nazi foreign ministry documents, many signed by Ribbentrop himself. Out of around 400 tonnes of paperwork, 60 documents directly related to the Duke of Windsor, most of which remained secret until their official release in 1996.

OPERATION WILLI

The most shocking revelation was a Nazi plot codenamed 'Operation Willi'. After the Second World War broke out the Duke of Windsor was awarded the rank of major general and was attached to the British Military Mission in France. However, following the invasion of France in 1940, the Windsors fled to Spain, where Edward made some hostile remarks about the royal family and Britain's role in the war, among other things. The couple then travelled to Portugal.

News of Edward's indiscreet statements reached Churchill and the prime minister ordered him to return to Britain. Because of his military rank Edward was reminded that if he disobeyed he would be court-martialled. There was then a change of plan. Increasingly viewed by the Allies as a liability who needed to be removed from Europe at all costs, the duke was hastily appointed governor of the Bahamas and ordered to assume his post at once. Somewhat unwillingly, the Windsors made their way to Lisbon to sail on the SS *Excalibur*.

By means of a plot code-named Operation Willi, the Nazis had planned to detain the Windsors before they sailed, with the intention of inducing Edward to work with the Nazi government in some way, perhaps by trying to reach a peace settlement with Britain. As a 'friend' of the regime – as Ribbentrop described him – the Duke of Windsor would then be restored to the throne after the Nazis had conquered England, as Hitler's puppet ruler. However, the plot failed and on 1 August 1940 the Windsors began their Atlantic crossing.

PUTTING HIS FOOT IN IT AGAIN

Even away from Europe, Edward could still embarrass the British government. In 1941, *Liberty* magazine published an interview in which he claimed that Hitler was 'the right and logical leader of the German people'. He also described Hitler as a 'great man', suggested that the war was being fought 'between two very stubborn peoples' and predicted that President Roosevelt would soon have to broker a peace agreement.

At the end of the war the Windsors returned to Paris, where they settled into a life of jet-setting celebrity until the Duke of Windsor's death in 1972. While we might suppose that the Duke of Windsor held fascist sympathies, we are unlikely to know for certain if he ever betrayed his country. What is clear, however, is that he spent a lifetime resenting the way in which he and his wife were treated by the British government and the royal household. In the end, the story of Edward and Mrs Simpson would be recast by many, not so much as a constitutional crisis but as one of the great romantic love sagas of the 20th century.

The Duke and Duchess of Windsor visit Germany against the advice of the government and meet up with Adolf Hitler in his Obersalzberg retreat, October 1937.

A TWIST IN THE TALE

Events in the life of Jeffrey Archer always seemed to be shrouded in mystery. His was a world where nothing could quite be taken at face value. Archer's reputation was such that when he was appointed deputy chairman of the Conservative Party in 1985, elder statesman Lord Whitelaw warned Prime Minister Margaret Thatcher that he was 'an accident waiting to happen'. It came as no surprise to some when a political career defined by turbulent peaks and troughs ground to a final halt in July 2001.

DUBIOUS CLAIMS

Archer first gained public attention as a talented athlete, gaining an Oxford blue as a sprinter and later representing Great Britain. Although he would claim his Oxford college as Brasenose, he was admitted to the far less exclusive Oxford University Department for Continuing Education, some biographies alleging that he gave false academic qualifications to gain entry. This is not the only time his past would be thrown into question: Archer claimed that his father was a decorated war hero when in fact he was a convicted fraudster who was alleged to have moved to the United States on his dead employer's passport.

Archer's networking skills made him an exceptional charity fundraiser. In 1964 he persuaded the Beatles to attend an Oxfam event he had organized at Brasenose, but Ringo Starr did not seem entirely sure about him. While visiting the public toilets, Starr quipped to another guest that 'he strikes me as a nice enough feller, but he's the kind of bloke who would bottle your piss and sell it'.

FROM MP TO NOVELIST

After two years in local government politics on the Greater London Council, in December 1969 Archer entered Parliament, winning a by-election for the seat in Louth, Lincolnshire.

At the age of 29 he was one of the youngest Members of Parliament. A popular local MP, his fledgling career was cut short by a financial scandal in 1974, when a fraudulent investment scheme involving a Canadian company called Aquablast left him half a million pounds in debt. Fearing bankruptcy, Archer stood down as an MP.

The resilient Archer bounced back with remarkable speed, reinventing himself as a dramatic novelist. Titles such as *Not a Penny More, Not a Penny Less* and *First Among Equals* may have been widely panned by literary critics but they were hugely popular with the public, not only in Britain but also in America, where *Kane and Abel* topped the *New York Times* bestsellers' list.

PAYS PROSTITUTE

There had been many attempts to lure Jeffrey Archer – by this time a high-profile public figure – back into front-line politics. Although he had no desire to return to Parliament, in 1985 he accepted the position of deputy chairman of the

Conservative Party. His brief time in the role was marked by controversy, but his resignation was eventually forced on 26 October 1986 when Britain awoke to a dramatic Sunday-morning headline in the *News of the World*: 'Tory Boss Archer Pays Vice Girl'. Michael Stacpoole, a friend and colleague of Archer, had arranged to meet prostitute Monica Coghlan at Victoria railway station to make a payment on his behalf. But Stacpoole was unaware that Coghlan was wired with two microphones and was being shadowed by a team of newspaper reporters. The grainy black and white front-page photograph showed Stacpoole handing over an envelope stuffed with £2,000 ($2,600) in £50 notes. It was given, the newspaper said, on the understanding that Coghlan would use it to leave the UK.

Lord Jeffrey Archer arrives at the Old Bailey shortly before being sentenced to four years' imprisonment for perjury and perverting the course of justice, relating to a previous trial against a British newspaper.

WINS DAMAGES

Six days later, the *Daily Star* ran its own take on the story, alleging that Archer had been one of Coghlan's clients and had paid her for sex – something the *News of the World* had only implied. Archer responded by suing the newspaper for libel. At the trial, his defence rested on the claim that the payment was entirely altruistic: it was, as his lawyer put it, the 'foolish act of a totally honourable man'. In his summing up, the judge, Mr Justice Caulfield, raised eyebrows as he drew attention to the testimony of Archer's wife, Mary, eulogizing her 'elegance' and 'fragrance'; his implication was clear – anyone with such a wife would scarcely

Jeffrey Archer and his fragrant wife Mary leave the courts during his libel case against the Daily Star in 1987. Archer won £500,000 in damages.

be in need of a prostitute. Archer won the case and was awarded £500,000 ($650,000) damages, at that time an unprecedented amount in Britain. He declared it a great victory and said he would give the money to charity. In the end, however, the *Daily Star* libel case would bring about his final downfall.

RECEIVES PEERAGE

Vindicated by the courts, Archer continued to be a high-profile figure within the Conservative Party and in 1992 he received a peerage from Prime Minister John Major in recognition of his charitable work. He took the title Lord Archer of Weston-super-Mare. But controversy continued to surround him and in 1994 he was investigated for insider dealing; he had made a £78,000 ($101,000) profit for a friend by buying and selling the shares of a company of which his wife was a director. No charges were brought.

Towards the end of the 1990s his political ambitions were rekindled as he declared an interest in standing for the newly created electoral post of Mayor of London. He assured party chairman Michael Ancram that no further allegations about his private or business life would resurface and in October 1999 he became the Conservative Party's official candidate. But barely a month later his political career was over.

IMPRISONED FOR PERJURY

On 21 November 1999, the *News of the World* published allegations by a former friend, television producer Ted Francis, that he had helped Archer commit perjury during the *Daily Star* libel case. Archer stood down from the mayoral election the following day and he was expelled from the Conservative Party for five years. There was worse to come.

Investigating the allegations in print, Detective Superintendent Geoff Hunt of Scotland Yard decided there was a legal case to answer, so Archer was charged with perjury and perverting the course of justice. In court, Ted Francis claimed that Archer had asked him to provide an alibi for the night he was supposed to have been with Monica Coghlan, and that together they had 'cooked up' a story that they were dining together at a London restaurant. The key witness in the case was Archer's former personal assistant, Angela Peppiatt, who told the court that Jeffrey and Mary Archer largely led 'separate lives' and that Archer had a long-standing mistress – another former PR, Andrina 'Andi' Colquhoun. Peppiatt painted a picture of a serial adulterer: 'He certainly had quite a few women who came to the apartment who Andi did not know about.' She also testified that she had been instructed to forge Archer's diary, used in the libel case, to include the false alibi.

On 19 July 2001 Archer was found guilty of both charges and sentenced to four years' imprisonment. He served two years of his sentence in an open prison, during which time he wrote his memoir, *A Prison Diary*. He then returned the libel award won from the *Daily Star*, as well as £1.3 million ($1.69m) in legal fees and interest, and retired from public life.

Jeffrey and Mary Archer largely led 'separate lives' and Archer had a long-standing mistress.

SEX AND THE FOUNDING FATHERS

When the private lives of our politicians become public we absorb the dramas in all their salacious glory. We're appalled at the hypocrisy and we applaud when the powerful are levelled by their own hubris. As fans of the award-winning hip-hop musical *Hamilton* will be more than aware, political sex scandals in America really do go right back to the Founding Fathers.

THE ORIGINAL AMERICAN SCANDAL

In the summer of 1791, Secretary of the Treasury Alexander Hamilton, widely regarded as the father of American finance, began a year-long affair with 23-year-old Maria Reynolds. She had approached the married politician begging for help with money, claiming to have been abandoned and left destitute by her husband. This turned out to be untrue. The woman's husband, Peter Reynolds, had encouraged the liaison so he could extort blackmail payments from Hamilton. By the time the affair ended, Hamilton had paid Reynolds $1,300 in hush money (around $35,000/£27,000 now). Shortly afterwards, Reynolds and a colleague, Jacob Clingman, were arrested for defrauding the US government by claiming the unpaid wages of deceased war veterans.

Attempting to bargain his way out of trouble, Clingman contacted his former employer, congressman Frederick

The statue of Alexander Hamilton in front of the Treasury Building In Washington DC.

Muhlenberg, claiming that Reynolds had taken part in a scheme to use federal funds to illegally speculate in government securities – and that his partner was none other than Alexander Hamilton. When Muhlenberg questioned Hamilton, he denied the allegation but confessed his affair with Reynolds' wife. Since there was clearly no financial impropriety involved it was not necessary to take legal action against Hamilton, but the details were leaked to his hated political rival, Thomas Jefferson.

THOMAS JEFFERSON'S SLAVE CONCUBINE

The story became news in 1796, when political pamphleteer James T. Callender published an account of the affair along with the financial allegations. Hamilton rashly responded with a pamphlet of his own, *Observations on Certain Documents*, which contained a detailed admission of his adultery. Few believed him guilty of corruption and many admired his candour, but the 'Reynolds Pamphlet' humiliated his wife and damaged both his reputation and his presidential aspirations beyond repair.

Portrait of Alexander Hamilton by Thomas Hamilton Crawford.

Thomas Jefferson, meanwhile, had presidential ambitions of his own. Impressed with his damaging attacks on Hamilton, Jefferson engaged James T. Callender to denounce his presidential rival, the incumbent John Adams. When Jefferson became president in 1801, Callender sought by way of reward the job of postmaster of Richmond, Virginia. Jefferson's refusal outraged Callender who responded with a series of savage personal newspaper articles in the *Richmond Recorder,* one of which alleged that President Jefferson, a widower for almost two decades, had kept 'as his concubine one of his own slaves' and was father to one of her children whose 'features are said to bear a striking although sable resemblance to those of the president himself'. The allegations were always denied but nonetheless sullied the reputation of one of America's greatest presidents. Following DNA analysis in 1998, it's now widely held as true that after the death of his wife Martha, Thomas Jefferson fathered at least five children with his slave Sally Hemings.

SERIAL SEX OFFENDER

One man who was definitely not an admirer of Thomas Jefferson was James Henry Hammond, a politician and plantation owner from the Deep South. During the American Civil War he was one of the most vociferous pro-slavery advocates.

'I firmly believe,' he said in 1845, while governor of South Carolina, 'that American slavery is not only not a sin, but especially commanded by God through Moses, and approved by Christ through his apostles.' He went on to say that: 'I repudiate, as ridiculously absurd, that much lauded but nowhere accredited dogma of Mr. Jefferson that "all men are born equal".'

There was no love lost between Alexander Hamilton and Thomas Jefferson, pictured here with laurel leaves.

At that time, of course, such views were not uncommon. Hammond, however, was also guilty of being a serial sex offender. Having married into a wealthy Confederate family, early in his marriage his brother-in-law, Wade Hampton II, discovered that Hammond had sexually abused his four daughters as teenagers. Hampton confronted Hammond, who admitted

African American slaves posed around a horse-drawn cart at a plantation on Edisto Island, South Carolina, 1862.

what he later referred to as his 'dalliances'. He found himself ostracized from his social circle and, in his words, the matter 'derailed his political career'. Hammond caused further consternation when his wife, Catherine ('a purer, more high minded and devoted woman never lived') discovered that he had repeatedly raped one of his female slaves, 18-year-old Sally Johnson; Hammond later raped her daughter, Louisa, first when she was just 12 years old. Both Sally and Louisa would bear a number of Hammond's children.

The full extent of his monstrous behaviour remained unknown until 1989 and the publication of *Secret and Sacred: The Diaries of James Henry Hammond, a Southern Slaveholder*. He detailed homosexual affairs (which truly would have been scandalous in the Deep South of the 19th century), made no attempt to defend the abuse of his teenage nieces – indeed he described their 'extremely affectionate' seductiveness as being to blame – and complained about the 'arrogance' of his wife and her family who 'think they have purchased me'. And he described his slaves, of whom he owned more than 300, as having no more value to him than his horses or mules. Hammond died in 1864, a year before the end of the Civil War. A Confederate to the end, he was purported to have instructed his son: 'If we [the South] are subjugated, run a plow over my grave.' History doesn't record whether or not Hammond Junior complied.

MURDERED BY HIS MISTRESS

Washington DC was the setting for one of the most dramatic of America's political sex scandals. On 8 December 1906 Utah Senator Arthur Brown was shot by his mistress, Anne

Maddison Bradley. Five days later he was dead. Stories of the tempestuous affair were well known in Salt Lake City, one newspaper simply declaring itself 'shocked but not surprised' at the news.

A successful Michigan lawyer, Brown was married with a child when he first became enamoured with senator's daughter Isabel Cameron. The affair caused a local scandal and he moved away to Utah, where he was able to marry his mistress after his divorce. In 1896 Brown was elected one of Utah's first senators. During the campaign, tongues began wagging when the 53-year-old Brown formed a 'close friendship' with Anne Bradley, 30 years his junior. In 1900 Bradley gave birth to their son, Arthur Brown Bradley.

Brown mainly lived apart from his wife at this time, although their reconciliations were evidently frequent. But Isabel Brown was aware of her husband's infidelity and hired a private investigator to shadow him and his mistress. In September 1902, Arthur Brown and Anne Bradley were charged with adultery after his wife claimed to have discovered more than 300 incriminating letters and telegrams. The two women eventually met and after a lengthy and violent argument each threatened to kill the other. Brown consequently gave Bradley a revolver for her protection – it would be the gun that she eventually used to kill him.

In August 1905 Isabel Brown died from cancer and Bradley assumed that the path would now be clear for her relationship with Brown to become official, but she was mistaken. With four children, and now pregnant with a fifth, Bradley requested money from Brown to set up a business. Although he agreed, he headed off to Washington DC for a court hearing before making any payment. Bradley pursued him, checking in at the same hotel. She went to his room only to find he was not there. Inside the room she found a number of love letters from an actress named Annie Adams Kiskadden, which seemed to be suggesting that she and Brown were planning to marry. When Brown returned to his room, the distraught Bradley took out the revolver and pulled the trigger. The *Washington Star* reported that 'she could not remember any of the events following'.

At the murder trial, Brown's will was read. 'I never married Anne M. Bradley and never intended to,' he declared. He furthermore specifically denied being the father to two of her sons and gave instructions that neither they nor Bradley should receive anything from his estate. The harsh words of Brown's will undoubtedly have swayed the jury and on 2 December 1907 Anne Bradley was acquitted. The case had painted a picture of an ill-treated, wronged woman who had been lied to and led on; there were few words of condolence for ex-Senator Brown.

Head and shoulders portrait of serial rapist J.H. Hammond, senator from South Carolina, who believed that slavery was sanctioned by God.

The Wolves of Wall Street outside the New York Stock Exchange in 2014 to mark the release of the DVD of the same name.

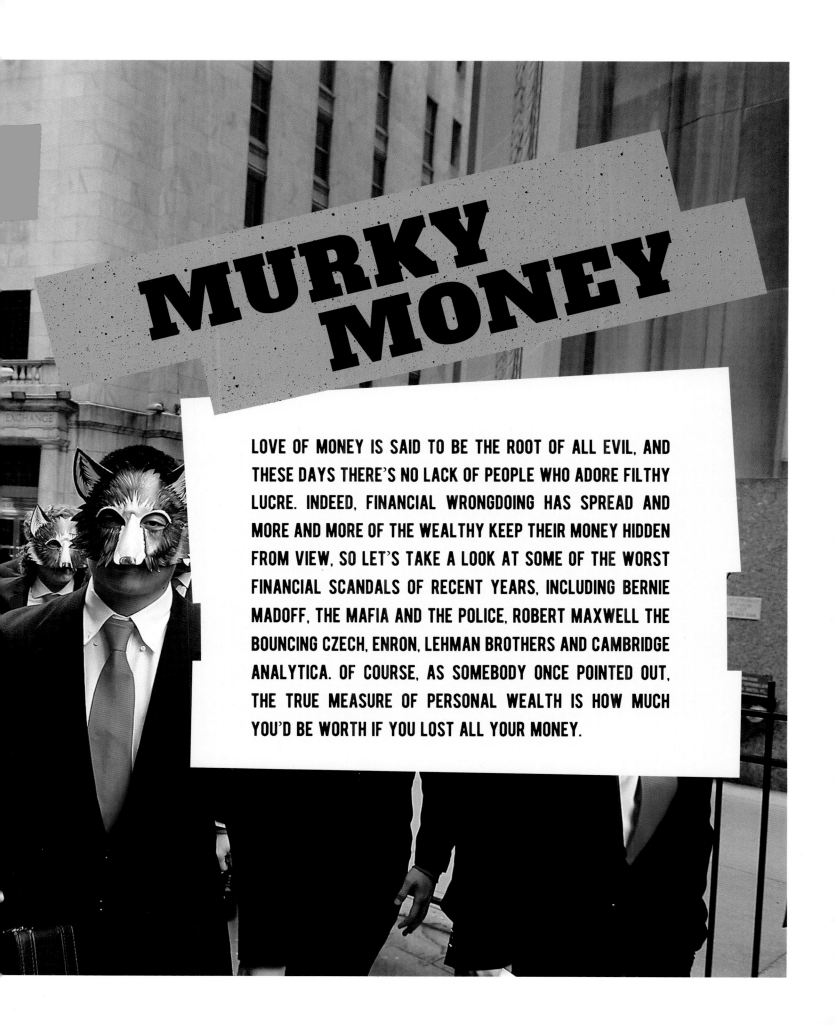

MURKY MONEY

LOVE OF MONEY IS SAID TO BE THE ROOT OF ALL EVIL, AND THESE DAYS THERE'S NO LACK OF PEOPLE WHO ADORE FILTHY LUCRE. INDEED, FINANCIAL WRONGDOING HAS SPREAD AND MORE AND MORE OF THE WEALTHY KEEP THEIR MONEY HIDDEN FROM VIEW, SO LET'S TAKE A LOOK AT SOME OF THE WORST FINANCIAL SCANDALS OF RECENT YEARS, INCLUDING BERNIE MADOFF, THE MAFIA AND THE POLICE, ROBERT MAXWELL THE BOUNCING CZECH, ENRON, LEHMAN BROTHERS AND CAMBRIDGE ANALYTICA. OF COURSE, AS SOMEBODY ONCE POINTED OUT, THE TRUE MEASURE OF PERSONAL WEALTH IS HOW MUCH YOU'D BE WORTH IF YOU LOST ALL YOUR MONEY.

BERNIE MADOFF: PONZI KING

Bernard Madoff was one of Wall Street's most respected figures. Long a fixture on the New York social scene, he lived in a luxury $7 million (£5.4m) property on the fashionable Upper East Side, with holiday homes in Long Island and Palm Beach. He was celebrated as one of the city's great philanthropists, donating millions of dollars to hospitals and cancer charities, but he was also the perpetrator of one of the biggest financial scandals of all time.

DROP-OUT

Shortly after dropping out of law school in 1960, Bernie Madoff started his own securities firm using $5,000 (£3,850) he'd made as a lifeguard on Rockaway Beach during his college summers. His firm made markets, buying and selling securities and other assets. An early champion of innovative technologies, by the turn of the century Bernard L. Madoff Investment Securities was one of the largest market makers on Wall Street.

PONZI SCHEME

But in December 2008 Madoff confided to his chief financial officer, Frank DiPascali, that the company couldn't meet a $7 billion (£5.4bn) demand for redemptions. In the midst of the worst financial crisis since the 1929 Crash, nervous clients wanted to recall their investments, but there wasn't enough in the company coffers for them to be paid. It would soon be revealed that for 20 years Bernard Madoff had been operating fraud on an unthinkably grand scale. It would cost his investors an estimated $19 billion (£14.6bn) in total.

Madoff used a 'Ponzi scheme'. This is a financial scam named after Charles Ponzi, a racketeer who made a fortune in the 1920s by swindling gullible investors out of more than $20 million (£15.4m). Ponzi was by no means the originator of the idea; indeed, a similar scam was described by Charles Dickens in his 1844 story *Martin Chuzzlewit*. The principle is remarkably simple. Victims are lured with a promise of regular high-yield returns on their investment. They are led to believe that these payments are the result of legitimate business activities, but in truth they are merely being paid out of the money taken from other investors. So long as willing new investors continue to contribute new funds – or existing investors can be persuaded to stay in the game to earn even greater profits – the scam can work indefinitely. These schemes eventually unravel when – as Madoff found – the operator can no longer pay the promised returns. This usually ends up with the operator vanishing, having pocketed the remaining investment money.

Bernard Madoff was able to operate his own Ponzi scheme for so long mainly because he was such a well-connected, senior figure in America's finance industry. He'd played a key role in launching the NASDAQ exchange and sat on the board of the National Association of Securities Dealers. Madoff's modus operandi was simplicity itself. He took his investors' money, placed it in his business account at J. P. Morgan Chase and withdrew money from the account when investors requested redemptions. The payments were backed up by fake trade reports created by specially designed computer software. Madoff's reputation within the industry was such that he was able to attract a consistent stream of wealthy investors over a long period. By the time the scheme was uncovered, Madoff's personal wealth was assessed at $126 million (£97m), with a further $700 million (£539m) in business interests.

ANALYST DISCOVERS FRAUD

This was not to say that Madoff's crime was entirely unsuspected. In 1999, financial analyst Harry Markopolos was asked by a Boston investment firm to reverse-engineer

Bernie Madoff leaves federal court in New York, 10 March 2009. Two days later he pleaded guilty to a fraud that totalled nearly $65 billion (£50bn).

Mugshots of conman Charles Ponzi, erstwhile Boston 'financial wizard'.

Madoff's trading strategies and revenue streams to see if they could be duplicated. He was immediately suspicious.

'As we know,' he told *60 Minutes* on CBS News in 2009, 'markets go up and down, and his only went up ... Clearly impossible. You would suspect cheating immediately,' he continued. 'It took me five minutes to know that it was a fraud. It took me another almost four hours of mathematical modelling to prove that it was a fraud.'

Markopolos reported his findings to the Securities and Exchange Commission (SEC) in May 2000. In all, he made five separate submissions between then and April 2008, but each time he was ignored.

LIVES DESTROYED

Unable to make payments, Madoff realized the game was up. After confessing to his sons and close business associates, on 11 December 2008 Bernard Madoff handed himself over to federal prosecutors.

'There is no innocent explanation,' he confessed.

On 12 March 2009 the 71-year-old Madoff pleaded guilty to 11 counts of fraud, theft and money laundering, then on 29 June he was stripped of his assets and sentenced to 150 years in prison. At the hearing, some of his victims were given the opportunity to tell how their lives had been destroyed by the fraud. Many had lost their life savings and some, who had money in feeder funds, were not even aware that they had invested in Madoff's scheme until they received notifications from their financial advisers. On 9 November 2017, the US government announced that it would begin paying out $772.5 million (£595m) to more than 24,000 of Madoff's victims.

THE MAFIA AND THE POLICE

Much of what most of us know about organized crime in the United States comes from classic movies like *The Godfather* and *Goodfellas*. These tales usually take place among the Italian-American communities of New York and New Jersey, and are centred on the most infamous of all crime syndicates, the Mafia.

BIRTH OF THE MAFIA

It was post-feudal Sicily that saw the birth of what we would later know as the Mafia. The 'Cosa Nostra' ('our thing'), as they termed themselves, appeared in the middle of the 19th century on the west side of the island, where there was almost no formal police force in operation. Wealthy businessmen would recruit young men, usually thugs or criminals, to protect their interests and what emerged was a number of dominant families each 'governing' their own locale, whose wealth was often founded on crime.

ITALIAN IMMIGRATION TO US

Rural poverty was rife in the southern half of Italy at this time and between 1860 and 1920 almost five million Italians crossed the Atlantic in search of a new life. Unsurprisingly, it was the major shipping passenger ports – New York, Boston and New Orleans – that first saw the Mafia at work in the United States. In 1869, the *New Orleans Times* reported an 'infestation of well-known and notorious Sicilian murderers'.

The Mafia quickly began to forge links with the local police and politicians. They were popular at election times as they were able to provide paying candidates with a private security force they could use – legally or otherwise – against their opponents. 'Pocketing' key police officers also meant that their activities would not be

Sicily was the breeding ground for the Mafia, an organization that soon wrapped its tentacles around the world.

Al Capone aboard the heavily guarded train that took him off to prison.

obstructed by the law, enabling them to gain a significant hold over protection and extortion rackets, gambling and prostitution within America's major cities.

It was the succession of the Fascists in Italy and the passing of the Prohibition laws in the United States that saw the Mafia families reach new heights of power and influence. When Benito Mussolini took control of Italy at the start of the 1920s, he immediately clamped down on Mafia activities, resulting in a second wave of immigration to the United States. With legitimate work hard to find, many Italians were quickly recruited into crime syndicates. Meanwhile, alcohol became outlawed in America and the Italian Mafia families waged frequent violent wars among themselves to gain control over the lucrative bootlegging markets. Prohibition saw infamous mobsters like Al Capone in Chicago achieving unthinkable wealth – his operation was thought to have brought in more than $100 million a year. (More than $1.2 billion (£920m) today.)

POLICE BRIBES

Capone and his men were able to operate unhindered due to his hold over the Chicago police force. A third of a bootlegger's revenue would typically be used to pay police bribes. Police warned of raids on speakeasies or warehouses in advance and murders of rival mobsters would be ignored – Capone was said to have ordered more than 500 killings.

Capone himself once said: 'I got nothing against the honest cop on the beat. You just have them transferred someplace where they can't do you any harm.'

When he was finally convicted in 1931 – on income tax charges – Chicago's chief of police claimed that 60 per cent of the force was on Capone's payroll. Ordinary police officers on a salary of $4,000 (£3,100) were found to have hundreds of thousands of dollars in their bank accounts. And the extortion extended to the very top, as the Attorney General, Harry Daugherty – the highest law officer in the country – was also found to be taking bribes.

Police corruption was widely reported and became a national scandal, with many complaining that the situation had been created by Prohibition. When the law was repealed in 1933 the Mafia was forced to look to other areas of criminal activity, such as narcotics, illegal sports gambling and financial fraud, often using restaurants and bars as a front.

LAW ENFORCEMENT VICTORIES

The first major law enforcement victory over the Mafia came in 1957, when police raided a historic summit of Mafia families being hosted on the estate of Joseph 'Joe the Barber' Barbara in Apalachin, New York. Fifty-eight mafiosi were arrested, resulting in 20 convictions for conspiracy. FBI director J. Edgar Hoover had always publicly denied the existence of the Mafia or any other national crime syndicate, but the publicity surrounding the Apalachin arrests ensured that more had to be done to keep the Mafia families under control. Key knowledge about the inner workings of the Mafia came from the 1963 state testimony of Joe Valachi, a low-ranking member of the Genovese – one of New York's infamous 'Five Families'.

The televised Valachi hearings gave the American public its first glimpse of the day to day functioning of the 'Cosa Nostra', the family hierarchies and the degree to which the bribery of officials had made their crimes possible.

RICO ACT

Valachi's disclosures played an important role in the creation of the Racketeer Influenced and Corrupt Organizations Act (RICO), which gave the law enforcement authorities significantly more power to investigate and prosecute mobsters.

The Mafia crime families are still active – most notably in New York and Chicago – but the RICO act would prove significant in curbing the advance of their power and influence. By the end of the 20th century, well over 1,000 Mafia mobsters had been convicted and countless others had broken traditional codes of silence by exchanging incriminating information for immunity from prosecution.

Ultimately, it would be the changing demographics of Italian-Americans that would seal the demise of the Mafia. Many of the younger generation that came from these once insular neighbourhoods – the Mafia's traditional recruiting ground – were now receiving college educations and assimilating into middle-class American society.

American mobster Joe Valachi testifies before the Senate Rackets Committee in Washington, 1963.

THE BOUNCING CZECH

On Tuesday 5 November 1991, the routine daily hubbub of Britain and America's newsrooms shifted into overdrive as news began to emerge that media mogul Robert Maxwell – owner of the *Daily Mirror*, the *Sunday Mirror*, the *People*, the *Daily Record*, the *New York Daily News* and a raft of other international newspaper titles and publishing houses – was missing.

MAN OVERBOARD

The reports were suggesting that Robert Maxwell had fallen overboard while sailing around the Canary Islands in his £15 million ($19.5m), 55-metre superyacht, *Lady Ghislaine*. Twelve hours later, 20 miles (32 km) south-west of Gran Canaria, a Spanish fisherman spotted Maxwell's naked body floating in the Atlantic.

ON THE VERGE OF COLLAPSE

... it seemed that some of the worst suspicions had been correct.

Prime Minister John Major described the flamboyant businessman, once one of the richest men in the world, as 'a great character', but others were less charitable. Rumours of dodgy dealings and questionable practices had swirled around since the 1960s. The fact that his businesses were run through a holding company in Liechtenstein made many of the allegations difficult to investigate, as did the legal web he had spun around himself. Teams of lawyers were retained and negative voices were always likely to find themselves under threat of a libel action. Now it seemed that some of the worst suspicions had been correct, for the immediate aftermath of Maxwell's death revealed a business empire on the verge of collapse, with further dramatic financial revelations imminent. The death of 'Cap'n Bob' or 'The Bouncing Czech', as detractors liked to

Robert Maxwell was a larger-than-life character who stayed afloat through complex financial wheeler-dealing.

call him, might have looked like an unfortunate accident, but some were openly speculating that the beleaguered tycoon may have taken his own life.

EARLY ADVERSITY

For Maxwell's family and those close to him, the idea that this could have been a suicide was unthinkable. He had, after all, led a dramatic life where adversity was certainly no stranger. Five decades earlier, most of his family had perished at Auschwitz after his country was occupied by the Nazis, but Ján Ludvík Hyman Binyamin Hoch made his way to France – assuming the name Ivan du Maurier – where he joined the Czechoslovak army in exile in 1940. After the defeat of France, he crossed the English Channel, where he enlisted in the British Army. A distinguished war career saw him rise from the rank of private to captain and he received the Military Cross from Field Marshal Montgomery. After the war he became a naturalized British citizen and in 1948 changed his name by deed poll to Ian Robert Maxwell.

NEWSPAPER MOGUL

Maxwell quickly thrived in business, turning a small scientific book company into a major publishing house, Pergamon Press. He also enjoyed a brief career in politics after entering Parliament as a Labour Party MP in 1964, retaining his seat until the 1970 general election. In 1969, Maxwell attempted a hostile takeover of Britain's most popular Sunday newspaper, the *News of the World*. Horrified that a Czech immigrant with socialist sympathies might take control of the paper, it ran an aggressive editorial proclaiming: 'This is a British paper run by British people ... Let us keep it that way!' A year later it was sold to Australian entrepreneur Rupert Murdoch. The two tycoons would remain lifelong foes.

PENSION SCANDAL

By the time of his death, Maxwell owned more than 400 companies on both sides of the Atlantic, but the extent of his financial decline was only then beginning to emerge, as was the astonishing way in which he'd attempted to keep it covered up. With more than $2 billion (£1.54bn) of debts, Maxwell began juggling both public and private assets, arranging costly and questionable deals in which he would pay other parties – such as Goldman Sachs – to buy stock in his companies. Most shockingly, he had diverted millions of pounds from the pension funds of his businesses to prop up the stock prices of his publicly held companies, Mirror Group Newspapers and Maxwell Communication Corporation.

'This is a British paper run by British people ... Let us keep it that way!'

Unsurprisingly, when the pension scandal broke it was Maxwell's biggest rivals that crowed the loudest. 'Crook of the Century' was emblazoned across the front pages of Rupert Murdoch's *Sun* newspaper. For this was more than an arcane story of City and Wall Street types mysteriously shuffling around enormous numbers at the behest of the monumentally wealthy. Here there were catastrophic repercussions for tens of thousands of Maxwell's rank and file employees, past and present.

THE BOUNCING CZECH 99

MAXWELL BROTHERS CHARGED

Maxwell's sons, Kevin and Ian, were left to run the company, but their father's business empire would nonetheless collapse beneath £3.4 billion ($4.4bn) of debt. After an eight-month inquiry by the Serious Fraud Squad, the Maxwell brothers were charged with one of the largest frauds in British history. Controversially, they were acquitted, leaving serious questions about who, precisely, would be held accountable for the £460 million ($598m) hole in the company pension funds.

In the end, a number of City of London institutions – among them Goldman Sachs and Lehman Brothers – would eventually agree to pay compensation of £276 million ($359m); but more than £100 million ($130m) was permanently lost.

In the light of those subsequent revelations, it's not difficult to picture the timing of Robert Maxwell's death as more than a coincidence. After all, as the *New York Times* reported: 'When he went to his boat on October 31, he had to know that the game was practically up.'

Easy does it: Robert Maxwell steps off his boat, Lady Ghislaine, *in 1991.*

WHEN ACCOUNTANTS TURN BAD

Scandals from the world of accountancy have rarely provided the sexiest of news headlines. They're often faceless, dry and lacking in drama and the details are too complex for most of us to comprehend. At the start of the 20th century, however, two unprecedented corporate collapses shocked America and dramatically affected the lives of thousands. Both were a consequence of rogue accountancy practices.

CREATION OF ENRON

Enron was founded in 1985 when Houston Natural Gas was merged with InterNorth, a natural gas company from Omaha, Nebraska. Its mission, as outlined by CEO Kenneth Lay, was to become 'the premier natural-gas pipeline in America'. The merger created a 37,000-mile (60,00,000 km) pipeline and over the next five years Enron began adding petroleum and power plants to its business portfolio. By 2000 Enron had become a colossus of global energy. *Fortune* magazine had named it 'Most Innovative Company' in America for the previous five years, the share price had reached an all-time high of $90 (£69) and the company was worth an estimated $60 billion (£46bn). Enron rode the nineties triumphantly: it was America's fifth-largest company and the world's biggest energy trader. It looked unstoppable.

The brains behind the growth of Enron had been Jeffrey Skilling. Initially hired as a management consultant, Skilling took advantage of deregulation within the industry to become an energy broker. The Gas Bank, as he named it, bought natural gas from producers at low prices and sold it on to consumers via fixed-price, long-term contracts. It was particularly effective in developing countries where both risk and margin were high and soon Enron had built power plants in Europe, Asia and Central America. Having begun as a rather traditional gas company, drilling and transporting energy, by 2000 97 per cent of Enron's income came from trading energy.

COOKING THE BOOKS

Hidden behind this rapid corporate ascent, however, was one problematic fact: too many of Enron's global ventures were disastrous commercial failures. Because the corporate ethos dictated that the share price was the only figure that truly mattered, it was crucial that these failures had to be buried. And this was achieved through what is known as 'mark-to-market' accounting, where the value of an asset is listed at its current market value rather than its book value. So a new venture would be listed immediately on the books based on its projected profit; if it failed to meet that projected profit, rather than being shown as a loss on the books it would be transferred to one of a number of Enron's dubious off-the-books 'partnerships'. In this way, any such losses would be unreported to Enron shareholders.

STOCK COLLAPSES

This kind of juggling accountancy could clearly only go on for so long before the whole operation imploded. Before that could happen, Kenneth Lay, Jeffrey Skilling and other senior Enron executives cashed in on their stock options while the share price was peaking, offloading their stock at just over $90 while at the same time advising investors that it was likely to rise beyond $130 (£100). Lay alone sold stock to the value of $70 million (£54m) and

Jeffrey Skilling arrives in court to find out how much longer he will have to stay in prison for his part in the fraud that destroyed the world's largest energy trader.

in total the Enron executives cashed in $600 million (£462m) worth of stock options. The rank and file employees were less fortunate; their shares were tied up in their company pensions and they could only watch on in horror as Enron stock collapsed to below $1 on 28 November 2001. Four days later the company was declared bankrupt and 4,500 jobs were lost.

PROSECUTIONS

Prosecutions took a considerable time to action, not reaching court until January 2006. After a 56-day trial, the jury rendered its verdict on 26 May and sentencing took place on 23 October. Kenneth Lay was found guilty on six counts of securities and wire fraud. He could have faced up to 45 years in prison had he not died from a heart attack before sentencing took place. Jeffrey Skilling was found guilty on counts of conspiracy, insider trading, making false statements to auditors and securities and wire fraud. He was sentenced to 24 years and four months in prison and was ordered to pay $630 million (£485m) to the government, which included a $180 million fine. His sentence was later reduced and he was released from custody in February 2019. In all, 21 people either pleaded or were found guilty in connection with the collapse of Enron. Additionally, Arthur Andersen – formerly one of the 'big five' corporate accountants – was effectively put out of business by its own involvement in the scandal.

The real losers were the former Enron employees. In May 2004, a class action won $85 million (£65m) compensation for the $2 billion (£1.54bn) lost from their pension funds, which was worth around $3,000 per employee. Enron shareholders were more fortunate, as

WorldCom's Bernie Ebbers arrives for sentencing with his wife Kristie in New York, 13 July 2005. Ebbers was an ex-milkman and bouncer who built a small Mississippi telephone company into the second-largest long-distance provider.

they were paid compensation of $7.2 billion (£5.54bn), largely from global banks which were said to have aided and abetted the fraud.

At the time it happened in 2001, Enron's downfall was the largest corporate failure in American history and by some distance the worst ever accountancy scandal. Until a year later. And WorldCom.

WORLDCOM ACCOUNTANCY FRAUD

One of America's major telecommunications suppliers, WorldCom was founded in 1983 and rapidly expanded by acquiring other telecoms companies. In 1997 it underwent a $37 billion (£28.5bn) merger with MCI, the largest in US corporate history, and by the end of the decade it was America's second-largest long-distance telephone company (after AT&T). But within two years WorldCom would file for Chapter 11 bankruptcy, after a $3.8 billion (£2.92bn) fraud had been uncovered.

Unlike Enron, the accountancy practices carried out at WorldCom were hardly sophisticated. It really was a simple fraud. In the early 21st century, the telecommunications market had become flooded and an excess of suppliers had resulted in a fall in consumer prices.

WorldCom had already signed long-term contracts with a number of third-party telecoms companies and now it was costing the company more to supply its services than was being received in revenue.

To hide falling profitability from shareholders, CEO Bernard Ebbers, CFO Scott Sullivan and other executives began the practice of taking operating expenses – such as interconnection costs with telecoms partners – and reclassifying them as capital expenditure on the balance sheet. This provided an exaggerated level of profitability and protected WorldCom's share price.

PERSISTENT AUDITORS

The fraud might have remained undetected without the dogged work of WorldCom's internal auditors. Growing suspicious of certain accounting entries, Cynthia Cooper recalled: 'The more we investigated, the stranger the reactions from some of our colleagues became. No one would give us a straight answer.' She and her team then began their own covert investigation, working secretly late at night, and quickly discovered $3.8 billion (£2.92bn) in fraudulent revenues posted between 1999 and 2002.

With the US Securities and Exchange Commission (SEC) investigating WorldCom's accountancy practices, CEO Ebbers resigned on 30 April 2002. The scandal became public on 25 June 2002 when the scale of the fraud was announced. CFO Scott Sullivan was then dismissed and two months later he was arrested. In July 2002, WorldCom filed for bankruptcy at a cost of 30,000 jobs and $180 billion (£138bn) to investors.

Bernard Ebbers received a 25-year jail sentence for his role in the fraud. In 2009 *Time* magazine listed him as the tenth-most-corrupt CEO of all time. Scott Sullivan was arrested on seven counts of fraud and after plea bargaining he received a five-year jail sentence in exchange for testifying against Ebbers. He was released in August 2009.

LEHMAN BROTHERS

If there's one enduring image of the 2008 financial crisis it is perhaps the photograph of the Lehman Brothers nameplate being ignominiously removed from its Wall Street offices. The fourth-largest investment bank in the United States, Lehman Brothers Holdings had been in existence for 158 years. Yet on 15 September 2008 a Chapter 11 bankruptcy petition was filed, citing a record $639 billion (£492bn) in debts. It remains the biggest corporate failure in history and it brought the world's financial system close to collapse.

SUBPRIME MORTGAGES

To figure out how a bank the size of Lehman could fail we need to understand its main business activity – subprime mortgages – and how these were linked to the financial markets. Mortgage funding was traditionally a self-contained process whereby the bank lent money to the home buyer using the deposits from their customers. This limited the number of mortgages that could be given out and made the banks treat applicants with a degree of caution.

It also limited the bank's profitability. The turn of the 21st century saw banks turning to the bond markets when offering mortgages. As far as the home buyer was concerned, this was all relatively transparent. The bank would sell the mortgage on the bond markets and when the home buyer paid the bank the bondholders would be reimbursed. This enabled banks to fund a far greater number of mortgages than would otherwise have been possible.

So lenders began offering packages to riskier customers, those with undocumented incomes or poor credit histories. These were called subprime mortgages. With property prices continually rising in the United States – peaking at 14 per cent year-on-year in 2005 – subprime mortgages were low risk and hugely profitable. So much so that mortgage brokers were urged to sell them in preference to standard mortgages. Subprime mortgages were particularly appealing because the interest was fixed at an artificially low rate for the first two years but threafter became linked to federal interest rates. By 2005, more than 20 per cent of all mortgages in America were subprime.

Lehman Brothers had invested heavily in the US property boom, acquiring five mortgage lenders by 2003, including the subprime specialists BNC and Aurora. They immediately yielded record revenues, surging 56 per cent from 2004 to 2006, and in 2007 the firm reported a record net income of $4.2 billion (£3.2bn) on revenues of $19.3 billion (£14.8bn).

WAVE OF REPOSSESSIONS

The problems began in 2006 when federal interest rates started to rise, hitting many subprime mortgage holders hard. In the following year there was a sudden surge in foreclosures. The wave of repossessions had a dramatic impact on house prices, which by the end of the year had fallen by around 10 per cent. From this position, the knock-on effects were catastrophic. Holders of subprime mortgages couldn't make their payments so the bondholders couldn't be paid. This naturally impacted any institution that had bought subprime mortgage bonds, such as pension funds.

Lehman Brothers' former chairman and CEO Richard Fuld (l) and Weil, Gotshal and Manges Business and Restructuring Partner Harvey Miller are sworn in before testifying to the Financial Crisis Inquiry Commission, 1 September 2010.

The US government could not afford to allow other huge banks to collapse.

LEHMAN'S BANKRUPTCY

The year 2007 was tumultuous for the financial markets. Lehman Brothers stock fell sharply in August and the subprime crisis grew so great that BNC and Aurora were closed down. By this time Lehman's leverage – the ratio of total assets to shareholders' equity – had risen to 31 and the size of its portfolio made it vulnerable to a market downturn. When Bear Stearns, the second-largest mortgage securities underwriter, came close to collapse in March 2008 Lehman shares fell by 48 per cent overnight. At the start of September, amid plunging global equity markets, Lehman stock collapsed. With only $1 billion (£770m) left in cash, it looked as if Lehman might be rescued by Barclays bank in London, but the move was vetoed by the Bank of England. In spite of its size and international status, the US government took what was seen as a controversial decision to let Lehman fail.

Overnight, the Dow Jones closed just over 500 points down, the largest drop since the Twin Towers attack on 11 September 2001, falling even more dramatically over the following week. Lehman's bankruptcy also had a catastrophic impact on the world's financial markets and proved to be the tipping point of a global recession. The US government could not afford to allow other huge banks to collapse and on 3 October President Bush announced a $700 billion (£539bn) bailout bill to save the Fannie Mae and Freddie Mac mortgage companies, Bear Stearns and AIG, as well as its 'big three' automobile manufacturers. In the UK, the government injected £37 billion ($48bn) of new capital into the Royal Bank of Scotland, Lloyds TSB and HBOS to avert the collapse of the financial sector.

MISLEADING ACCOUNTANCY PRACTICES

The public face of the Lehman collapse was CEO Richard 'The Gorilla' Fuld, who was typically bullish in his assessment. 'This is a pain that will stay with me for the rest of my life,' he declared. He also placed the blame with the politicians who had encouraged looser lending standards and homeowners who used their properties 'like an ATM'. In 2009, the Condé Nast investment magazine *Portfolio* listed Fuld as number one on their 'Worst American CEOs of All Time' list.

In 2010, an official report on the Lehman bankruptcy noted what it called 'materially misleading' accountancy practices intended to mask the true state of the company's finances. During the months leading up to its final collapse, Lehman had used an accounting technique called REPO 105 to temporarily move $50 billion (£38bn) of its assets into cash to conceal its heavy dependence on leverage – borrowed money. The accounts had been signed off by Fuld and certified by Ernst & Young, Lehman's external auditors. New York's Attorney General, Andrew Cuomo, filed a lawsuit against Ernst & Young for negligence, seeking more than $150 million (£115m) in fees they had been paid between 2001 and 2008. The case was settled for $10 million (£7.7m) plus the costs of the investigation. And in 2013 Ernst & Young would settle a class action lawsuit with Lehman's investors for $99 million (£76m). In both cases, there was no admission of wrongdoing. Although widely viewed as culpable, neither Dick Fuld nor any other Lehman executives faced prosecution.

DATA MINING: A 21ST CENTURY SCANDAL

A very modern scandal, at first glance the 2018 Cambridge Analytica controversy might have seemed too arcane to interest the world's media. It certainly brought the terms 'data harvesting' and 'psychographic profiling' into the mainstream, even if most people responded with a shrug of the shoulders after realizing that this didn't in fact mean their online accounts had been hacked. Yet as the scandal unfolded, it became increasingly clear just how powerful the results of highly sophisticated digital targeting could be to an organization and how wide-ranging the implications might be – even affecting the future of our democratic processes.

HOW IT WORKED

Founded in 2013, Cambridge Analytica's business was to take detailed social media and polling information and use it to target potential voters in elections. Owned in part by politically conservative American hedge fund manager Robert Mercer, it would contribute to a wide variety of political races in the United States during 2014. Cambridge Analytica would also provide analysis for Donald Trump's presidential campaign and Leave.EU, one of the lobbying groups backing Britain's exit from the European Union during the 2016 referendum.

On the surface, these activities all seem to have been completely legal. But in March 2018 both the *New York Times* and the *Observer* newspapers broke reports that shed new light on some of Cambridge Analytica's business practices. Implicated in these activities was the biggest social media phenomenon of them all: Facebook.

Cambridge Analytica CEO Alexander Nix arrives to give evidence to Parliament's Digital, Culture, Media and Sport Committee, 6 June 2016.

FACEBOOK DATA PROFILES GENERATED

The man who revealed what had been happening was a Canadian data analyst named Christopher Wylie, who had been employed as a contractor by London-based SCL Elections, Cambridge Analytica's parent company. He revealed how Cambridge University data scientist Aleksandr Kogan had created a Facebook app for Cambridge Analytica called 'thisisyourdigitallife'. A paid detailed personal survey, its intended use seemed to be to mine data from several hundred thousand Facebook subscribers for academic use. It also took advantage of Facebook's loose approach to data security: if you gave permission via the app to access your own personal Facebook data, it also provided access to your entire friend network.

In this way, the 270,000 Facebook users who completed the 'thisisyourdigitallife' quiz were responsible for generating data profiles for around 87 million other Facebook users. Since the data also included location information, Cambridge Analytica would be able to create detailed psychographic profiles that could be used for very precise digital targeting during an election campaign. This meant that specific content – news stories (or fake news stories) – could subtly find its way into the social media news feeds of people who had never given permission for their data to be accessed in the first place. There is plenty of disagreement as to how effective this practice really is – although it appears to be useful enough for wealthy organizations and individuals to plough millions of dollars into its use.

Christopher Wylie blew the whistle on Cambridge Analytica. Here he poses for his photo in Brussels, 26 November 2018.

WERE POLITICAL OUTCOMES INFLUENCED?

Further investigation unearthed a more traditional side of political campaigning, when undercover investigative videos were aired showing Cambridge Analytica CEO Alexander Nix boasting about how he could use prostitutes, sting operations and honey traps to discredit politicians. Following the media outcry the British High Court granted the Information Commissioner's Office a warrant to search Cambridge Analytica's London offices.

The scandal would be a severe embarrassment to Facebook, which banned Cambridge Analytica from using its services, claiming that it had been deceived. A contrite CEO Mark Zuckerberg made a public apology, calling it: 'a breach of trust between Kogan, Cambridge Analytica and Facebook ... also a breach of trust between Facebook and the people who share their data with us and expect us to protect it. We need to fix that.'

As for the source data, Alexander Nix and Aleksandr Kogan were in disagreement about responsibility. Nix claimed that his company had received the data from a 'seemingly reputable' contractor 'in good faith' and Kogan felt he had been made a scapegoat.

On 1 May 2018, Cambridge Analytica and its parent company filed for insolvency proceedings and closed operations. The big question that remained unanswered, however, was how much of an impact its use of illegally mined data had on the narrow election victories of both Donald Trump in America and the Brexit campaign in Britain – neither of which had been fully expected.

The Khalifa International Stadium under construction in 2016 in the Aspire Zone, Doha, Qatar, venue for the FIFA World Cup Final 2022.

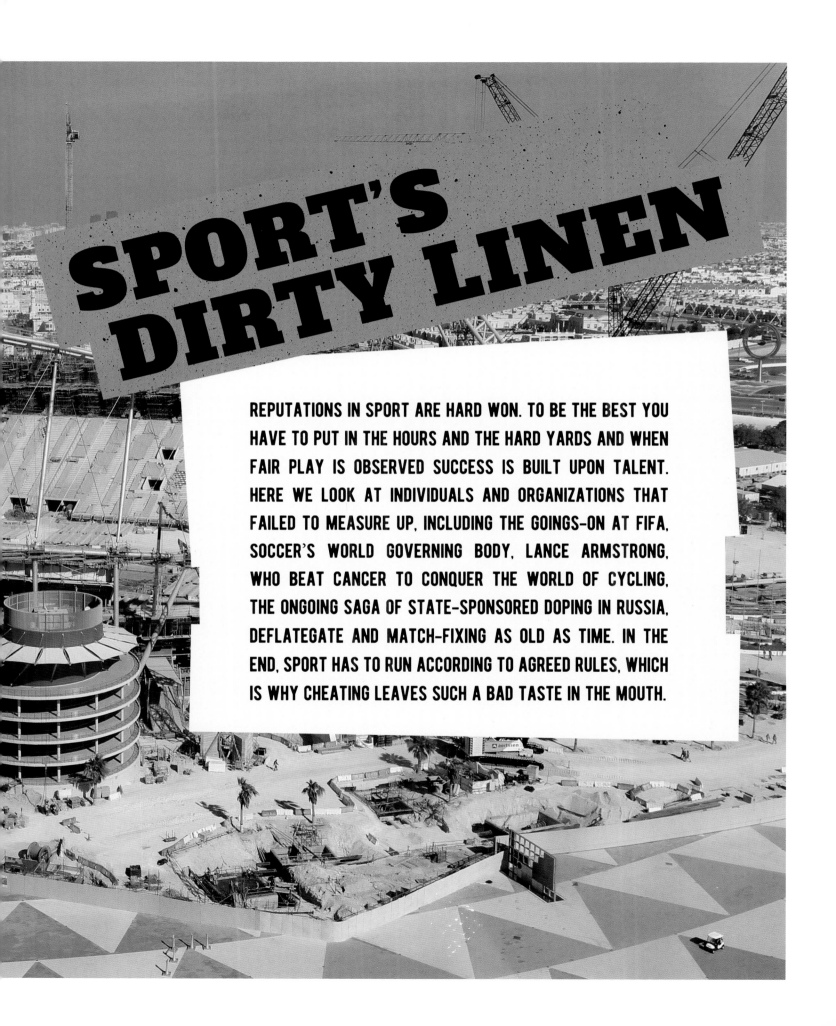

SPORT'S DIRTY LINEN

REPUTATIONS IN SPORT ARE HARD WON. TO BE THE BEST YOU HAVE TO PUT IN THE HOURS AND THE HARD YARDS AND WHEN FAIR PLAY IS OBSERVED SUCCESS IS BUILT UPON TALENT. HERE WE LOOK AT INDIVIDUALS AND ORGANIZATIONS THAT FAILED TO MEASURE UP, INCLUDING THE GOINGS-ON AT FIFA, SOCCER'S WORLD GOVERNING BODY, LANCE ARMSTRONG, WHO BEAT CANCER TO CONQUER THE WORLD OF CYCLING, THE ONGOING SAGA OF STATE-SPONSORED DOPING IN RUSSIA, DEFLATEGATE AND MATCH-FIXING AS OLD AS TIME. IN THE END, SPORT HAS TO RUN ACCORDING TO AGREED RULES, WHICH IS WHY CHEATING LEAVES SUCH A BAD TASTE IN THE MOUTH.

BRIBES AND BUNGS: CORRUPTION AT FIFA

For almost four decades, Joseph 'Sepp' Blatter had been the central figure within the Fédération Internationale de Football Association (FIFA), the international governing body of the world's most popular sport. Then it all began to fall apart.

OPULENCE AND BRIBES

From his election as FIFA's general secretary in 1981 and beyond his presidency that began seven years later, Sepp Blatter was the undoubted mastermind behind soccer's rapid commercial dominance in virtually every corner of the world. Living the opulent life of a head of state, kings, presidents, sheikhs and prime ministers would be drawn to his fiefdom in Zurich, all seeking the sport's ultimate prize – the right, once every four years, to stage the FIFA World Cup. For the chosen one, there was the prestige of hosting the month-long tournament, second in global viewership only to the Olympic Games. Little wonder, then, that potential hosts viewed the World Cup less as a football tournament than as a grand-scale public relations exercise. With so much at stake it came as little surprise to find that attempts to subvert the supposedly fair and transparent bidding process were commonplace ... and that behind the scenes large sums of money had been illegally changing hands. Bribes and 'bungs' were being used to buy or lobby for votes in key FIFA elections, money was being laundered and taxes were being evaded. It would take the dogged obsession of one journalist and the power of the FBI to bring about Sepp Blatter's fall from grace.

WHISTLE-BLOWER

Rumours of financial impropriety within FIFA had been rife for years, but it was British investigative journalist Andrew Jennings who first unearthed and published the evidence. As early as 2002 he had been contacted by a whistle-blower with allegations of widespread corruption. His findings were published in the *Sunday Times* newspaper and formed the basis of a 2006 BBC documentary, *The Beautiful Bung: Corruption and the World Cup*. Two years later Jennings was approached by the FBI, who were beginning their own investigations

using the Racketeer Influenced and Corrupt Organizations Act (RICO), originally introduced to fight the Mafia. (Indeed, Evan Norris, one of the eventual prosecutors, had previously convicted members of the Gambino Mafia family, and drew a number of parallels between the two organizations.)

AS the head of world football, Sepp Blatter was accused of many things.

VOTING PROCESS ALLEGATIONS

Suspicions were further raised on 2 December 2010, when Sepp Blatter announced the results of the bids for the 2018 and 2022 World Cup tournaments. Both were controversial: 2018 went to Russia, a country with high levels of racism associated with football which had also recently received global censure for the annexation of Crimea; and 2022 was awarded to Qatar, a state with an appalling human rights record, no footballing tradition and a local climate completely alien to the sport. Attention turned to the voting process when Jennings made a second film for the BBC. *FIFA's Dirty Secrets* was broadcast three days before the announcement and contained allegations that FIFA officials had been bribed for their votes. This was followed up in the *Sunday Times* amid reports that two committee members, Issa Hayatou and Jacques Anouma, had each been given $1.5 million (£1.16m) in exchange for voting in favour of Qatar.

BLANKET DENIALS

As would always be the case, the allegations were given blanket denials by Blatter, but the persistent public accusations led to FIFA commissioning former US Attorney General Michael Garcia to investigate 'ethical breaches' and other wrongdoings within the organization. In September 2014 the 350-page Garcia report was submitted to FIFA – which controversially refused to publish its findings. Instead, executive Hans-Joachim Eckert published his own 42-page summary in November, which was treated with derision by the media as a whitewash. Garcia himself called it 'materially incomplete' and resigned in protest.

Workers outside the Lusail Iconic Stadium in Qatar – many have asked how the World Cup finals could be held in such an extremely hostile climate.

The FBI investigation was not concerned with the matter of tournament hosting but corruption within CONCACAF and CONMEBOL, the two FIFA bodies that run football in North and South America respectively. They were particularly interested in allegations of racketeering, wire fraud and money laundering between FIFA executives, sports marketing firms and broadcasters. The breakthrough for the FBI came when CONCACAF general secretary Chuck Blazer, who was being investigated separately for income tax violations, agreed to take part

in covert operations. Hoping to avoid a potential lengthy prison sentence for racketeering, Blazer agreed to make secret audio recordings of meetings with other FIFA officials using a device built into his key ring. Blazer's evidence formed the basis of the FBI's investigation.

FIFA EXECUTIVES ARRESTED

A copy of the Garcia report had meanwhile been sent to Switzerland's Attorney General, who declared that there were 'grounds for suspicion ... which merit examination by the criminal prosecutions authorities'. On 27 May 2015, Swiss plainclothes police entered the five-star Baur au Lac Hotel, where FIFA's 65th annual congress meeting was being held, and arrested seven executives for extradition to the United States. Later that day, across the Atlantic in New York City, the Justice Department disclosed a 164-page, 47-count criminal indictment of 14 defendants who had received $150 million (£115m) in bribes over a period of two decades. A second indictment made in December 2015 listed a further 16 officials from CONCACAF and CONMEBOL, along with two other FIFA executives who were arrested in Zurich. Most of those convicted would later plead guilty; some cases are yet to be resolved.

BLATTER REMOVED FROM OFFICE

One name, however, was conspicuous by its absence: Sepp Blatter. In fact, two days after the Zurich bust he won a vote to continue as president of FIFA. He responded by promising that FIFA would be reformed and that he would 'continue to work with the relevant authorities ... to root out any misconduct'. However, his triumph was to be shortlived. With rumours that he was under personal investigation, along with the publication of an incriminating 2008 letter showing that he knew of a $10 million (£7.7m) payment from FIFA to disgraced former vice-president Jack Warner, Blatter announced his decision to step down ... after the next election.

> He responded by promising that FIFA would be reformed and that he would 'continue to work with the relevant authorities ... to root out any misconduct'.

While never admitting to any wrongdoing, Blatter was finally removed from office by FIFA's own ethics committee. On 17 September 2015, general secretary Jérôme Valcke was suspended by FIFA, accused of having been involved in a scheme to sell football tickets at inflated prices; a week later the head of UEFA (Europe's footballing body), former star footballer Michel Platini, was questioned about a $2 million (£1.54m) payment from Blatter. Although both claimed it was connected to Platini's FIFA pension, both were banned for eight years from taking part in any football-related activity.

In February 2016 Gianni Infantino was elected as the ninth president of FIFA. After an 'incredibly tough year', he declared with some understatement: 'I am committed to putting football back at the heart and soul of what our organisation does.' It remains to be seen if FIFA can – or even really wants to – reform itself.

THE GOLDEN BOY WHO LOST HIS SHEEN

The winner of seven Tour de France titles between 1999 and 2005, Lance Armstrong was regarded as the greatest road racing cyclist of his generation. What's more, his greatest successes followed a potentially fatal brush with cancer, an experience that led him to set up his own charitable foundation. He was nothing less than the golden boy of American sport.

CANCER DIAGNOSIS

Lance Armstrong began his professional road racing career with the Motorola team in 1992. He secured his first major victories at the age of 22 the following year, winning the UCI Road World Championship and finishing first in Stage 8 of the Tour de France.

In 1996, two months after signing a $2 million (£1.54m) sponsorship deal, Armstrong was struck down with a life-threatening cancer diagnosis: stage three testicular cancer had spread to his brain, lungs and abdomen. His urologist later revealed that prior to surgery he had thought that Armstrong had 'almost no hope' of survival, let alone resuming his career.

Armstrong's rapid recovery astonished the sports world. Declared free of cancer at the end of 1996, he joined the US Postal Service Pro Cycling Team in 1997 and began an intensive year of training. His comeback began in 1998 with a fourth place in the Vuelta a España. But it was in the following year that Lance Armstrong began his startling elevation to road racing legend. Between 1999 and 2005, he recorded no fewer than seven consecutive overall victories in the Tour de France, the world's most prestigious road race.

FIRST DOPING ALLEGATIONS

Along with his successes came rumour and suspicion. The first specific doping allegations came in 1999 as Armstrong won Stage 9 of the Tour de France. There was plenty of comment in the European media about the ease with which he was able to complete the notoriously brutal Alpine ascent. The same was true of Armstrong's relationship with controversial Italian coach Michele Ferrari. A qualified doctor, Ferrari had already sidestepped criminal charges in Italy for 'sporting fraud' and 'abuse of the medical profession'. He was widely criticized for making light of the suspected use in the sport of erythropoietin (EPO), a hormone that stimulates the production of red blood cells and thus improves the delivery of oxygen from the lungs to the muscles.

The first high-profile doping allegation involving Armstrong came in 2004, when the book *L.A. Confidentiel – Les secrets de Lance Armstrong* was published in France. It detailed claims by a former team assistant, Emma O'Reilly, that during his 1999 Tour victory – when Armstrong had tested positive for illegal steroid use – a compliant doctor had agreed to issue a back-dated prescription for a steroid cream used for treating saddle sores. She was also reported to have said that she had disposed of used syringes and also picked up 'mysterious parcels'. When the extracts from the book were published in English in the *Sunday Times* newspaper, Armstrong sued for libel. The matter was settled out of court.

Lance Armstrong waves to the crowd after the 20th and final stage of the Tour de France in 2010.

FROZEN URINE

The allegations continued in 2005, when French newspaper *L'Équipe* published a headline story *'Le Mensonge Armstrong'* ('The Armstrong Lie'). It reported that six urine samples frozen and stored during that same 1999 Tour de France had been retested and had shown traces of EPO. The World Anti-Doping Agency (WADA) demanded that cycling's world governing body, Union Cycliste Internationale (UCI), should launch an independent inquiry. A year later the report concluded that the samples had been improperly handled and couldn't be used as evidence. Referring to the article as part of an ongoing 'witch hunt', Armstrong's bullish response was that he had 'never taken performance-enhancing drugs'. There would later be suggestions that a large, six-figure charitable 'donation' by Armstrong to the UCI had influenced the outcome of the investigation, but this was always denied.

CRIMINAL INVESTIGATION

The following year, Bob Hamman, president of Dallas-based insurance company SCA Promotions, read the allegations made in *L.A. Confidentiel* and decided to withhold a $5 million (£3.85m) bonus payable to Armstrong following his sixth Tour victory. Hamman knew he would be forced to pay the bonus in the end but hoped that the testimonies would raise enough suspicion to trigger a further investigation – enabling SCA to sue for the return of their fee. As intended, officials from the United States Anti-Doping Agency (USADA) asked to review the evidence.

In 2010, federal prosecutors for the US Department of Justice began a criminal investigation into claims made by fellow cyclist Floyd Landis that doping was widespread among members of the US Postal Service Pro Cycling Team. He claimed he had witnessed Armstrong receiving blood transfusions and administering illegal testosterone patches to his teammates. A year later another former teammate, Tyler Hamilton, told the CBS *60 Minutes* news show that he and Armstrong had taken EPO before the 1999, 2000 and 2001 Tours.

As the evidence seemed to be stacking up against Armstrong, many were surprised when, without comment, the Department of Justice dropped the criminal investigation and declared that no charges would be brought. USADA, however, continued its investigation and on 10 October 2012 the damning verdict was delivered. In a 200-page report, with a further 1,000 pages of supporting documentation, chief executive Travis T. Tygart declared: 'The US Postal Service Pro Cycling Team ran the most sophisticated, professionalized and successful doping program that sport has ever seen.'

ALL TITLES STRIPPED

With specific regard to Armstrong, there was, he continued, 'direct documentary evidence including financial payments, emails, scientific data and laboratory test results that further prove the use, possession and distribution of performance-enhancing drugs by Lance Armstrong and confirm the disappointing truth about the deceptive activities of the USPS Team, a team that received tens of millions of American taxpayer dollars in funding.'

The USADA report would deal one final crushing blow: Armstrong was to receive a lifetime ban from the sport and all titles since 1 August 1998 were to be stripped from him – including his seven Tour de France titles. The UCI announced that they would not challenge the decision. In quick succession, Nike, Radio Shack, Anheuser-Busch, Trek Bicycle Corporation and other global corporations dropped their sponsorship deals. The final indignity came as he was forced to step down from his own cancer foundation.

Michele Ferrari shrugs at a hearing in Bologna – but did he help orchestrate an elaborate doping programme for Lance Armstrong?

PUBLIC APOLOGY

Lance Armstrong finally came clean in dramatic style. During a TV interview with Oprah Winfrey that aired over two nights in January 2013, he showed little emotion as he admitted to having routinely used banned performance-enhancing drugs during what he called 'the EPO era'. He further acknowledged that he had used blood doping, transfusions and human growth hormones.

With his sporting achievements now declared null and void, Lance Armstrong has effectively been removed from cycling's record books. But did Armstrong lose his reputation in vain? A study published in *The Lancet* in 2017 has come to the conclusion that the supposedly performance-enhancing drug EPO does not work.

Two groups of cyclists were administered either EPO or a placebo over a two-month period and neither group performed better than the other.

As Jules Heuberger of the Centre for Human Drug Research said: 'It's just tragic to lose your career for something that doesn't work.'

THE ROGUE STATE OF OLYMPIC DOPING

The 2018 Winter Olympic Games in Pyeongchang, South Korea, were notable for the large number of athletes taking part as 'neutrals' under the Olympic flag. Two months before the start of the competition, doping revelations had led the International Olympic Committee (IOC) to ban Russia from taking part in the tournament, marking the most dramatic punitive measure it had ever taken against a single nation. Although many other international athletes had in the past failed routine drug tests, Russia was much the worst offender. This was a nation where the use of performance-enhancing drugs (PEDs) had been endemic since the days of the old Soviet Union.

EARLY PERFORMANCE ENHANCEMENT

In the early days of the modern Olympic movement, methods for improving competitive performance were crude. When American marathon runner Thomas Hicks began flagging at the 1904 St. Louis Olympics, his assistant administered a near-fatal dose of strychnine and brandy as a pick-me-up. By the end of the 1950s, doping was becoming an increasingly sophisticated science, yet it was still not an outlawed practice. It was only after the death of Danish cyclist Knud Enemark Jensen at the 1960 Rome Olympics, caused by amphetamine use in 40°C (104°F) temperatures, that the IOC Medical Commission was founded. At the 1968 Winter Olympics in Grenoble, France, a list of banned substances was produced, along with the first official drug tests.

With drug testing technology still in its infancy during the 1970s, illegal doping became widespread and systematic in the Soviet Union and other Eastern Bloc states. It wasn't

The 2018 Winter Olympics in Pyeongchang, South Korea featured many athletes competing as neutrals under the Olympic flag.

until the fall of communism that the true extent of state-sponsored involvement was revealed: in former East Germany, documents showed that anabolic steroids had been routinely given to female swimmers and gymnasts as young as 11 years old. And it was revealed that the KGB had taken part in its own deceptions. Its agents had purportedly posed as IOC officials to tamper with urine and blood samples.

'THE CHEMISTS' GAMES'

The 1980 Summer Olympic Games in Moscow were a much-reduced affair. Following the Soviet invasion of Afghanistan, 66 states – led by the USA – boycotted the tournament. By this time, the use of testosterone and the anabolic steroid nandrolone had become widespread, especially since they could not easily be detected. Indeed, there was not a single positive drug test in the Moscow tournament. Alongside official tests, IOC scientist Manfred Donike ran his own private study, using a technique he had developed for detecting abnormal levels of testosterone. He found that more than 20 per cent of the samples he tested – including a number of medal winners – showed traces of banned substances hidden from the official tests.

The Soviet Union had, in fact, planned a state-wide doping programme in the run-up to the 1984 Los Angeles Olympics. A document made public in 2016, signed by Sergei Portugalov of the Institute for Physical Culture, detailed how nandrolone injections could be administered during training, but the drug would be undetectable as long as they were stopped around 150 days before the competition. The scheme became unnecessary when the Soviet Union and other Eastern Bloc states pulled out of the tournament altogether in retaliation for the 1980 boycott, but Dr Portugalov's name would emerge in later Russian doping scandals.

FORMATION OF WADA

Amid growing negative media headlines, the IOC sought more effective ways to combat the use of banned substances in sport. This initiative led to the formation of the independent World Anti-Doping Agency (WADA) in 1999. Individual nations also ran their own affiliated anti-doping facilities. In 2010, a staff member at the Russian Anti-Doping Agency (RUSADA), Vitaly Stepanov, began leaking details of the systematic use of PEDs among Russia's top athletes. More than 200 emails and 50 letters made their way to WADA over a three-year period. According to Stepanov, WADA had been reluctant to take action itself, and so passed on the incriminating data to an investigative reporter at the German broadcaster ARD. The resulting documentary, Hajo Seppelt's *The Doping Secret: How Russia Creates its Champions*, alleged that almost all of Russia's top athletes were involved in the use of PEDs. The most sensational claim was that Russian officials had offered banned substances in exchange for a percentage of the athlete's earnings, and that Russian anti-doping laboratories had been routinely falsifying documents. One of the central figures was said to be Dr Sergei Portugalov, by this time chief medical officer of the Russian Athletics Federation.

RUSSIAN DOPING OPERATION EXPOSED

In response to the documentary, WADA commissioned its own investigation, which in November 2015 reported 'a deeply rooted culture of cheating ... interference with doping controls ... cover ups, destruction of samples and payment of money to conceal doping tests'. The damning 335-page report concluded that RUSADA was operating under the influence of the Russian Ministry of Sport. It recommended that Russia should be barred from the 2016 Rio de Janeiro Olympics. Although WADA suspended RUSADA, the IOC decided against an outright ban.

In 2016, however, Grigory Rodchenkov, who had been director of an anti-doping laboratory in Moscow, fled to the United States and turned whistle-blower. Interviewed in May 2016 by the *New York Times*, he declared that at the 2014 Winter Olympics at Sochi, Russia, dozens of his nation's athletes – among them the 15 medal-winners – had taken part in a meticulously planned deception. Russian intelligence agents had initiated a daring late-night operation that saw tainted urine samples passed through a small hole in the laboratory wall and replaced with clean samples. WADA responded within days, commissioning an investigation by Canadian attorney Richard McLaren. His report concluded 'beyond a reasonable doubt' that RUSADA, the Ministry of Sport, the Federal Security Service and the Centre of Sports Preparation of the National Teams of Russia had operated 'a state-directed failsafe system' using what he called 'the disappearing positive test methodology'. But the IOC again refused to ban Russia from the Rio Olympics, although 43 Russian athletes who took part at Sochi did receive retrospective disqualifications, 13 being stripped of medals.

RUSSIA BANNED THEN REINSTATED

The scale of the scandal quickly developed a political dimension, with Russian president Vladimir Putin accusing the USA of deliberately attempting to isolate Russia's athletes. At the same time, the IOC also received widespread criticism of its reluctance to take a decisive stand on the matter. In November 2017, Grigory Rodchenkov – now claiming that his life was under threat from Russian agents – provided new evidence to the IOC, who finally announced the suspension of the Russian Olympic Committee. As a concession, Russian athletes with no drug violations would be allowed to compete at the 2018 Pyeongchang Winter Olympics under the Olympic flag; of 500 athletes nominated, only 169 were permitted to take part.

Shortly after the completion of the Winter Olympics in February 2018, the International Olympic Committee controversially announced that Russia would be reinstated. And the following September members of the World Anti-Doping Agency voted unanimously to reinstate the Russian Anti-Doping Agency. Grigory Rodchenkov declared the decision 'a catastrophe ... the greatest treachery against clean athletes'. Judging from the outrage expressed in the media, this would seem to be a view still held by many.

BBC journalist David Eades interviews Grigory Rodchenkov (seen on screen) on behalf of the Foundation for Sports Integrity, London, 31 May 2018.

DEFLATEGATE

The act of tampering with the ball to gain competitive advantage has always raised controversy in sport, blurring the lines between what constitutes fair play, gamesmanship or outright cheating. In the early days of baseball, it was quickly discovered that applying saliva or petroleum jelly to one side of the ball would alter the wind resistance, causing it to move through the air in an unexpected way so it was difficult to hit. 'Spitball', as it was called, had been a standard part of the game until it was banned in the 1920s.

UNDERINFLATED BALL REPORTED

Ball manipulation within the National Football League had never been a headline issue until 18 January 2015, when it was alleged that Tom Brady, a celebrated quarterback for reigning Super Bowl champions the New England Patriots, had ordered the deliberate deflating of balls used in his team's playoff victory over the Indianapolis Colts. It was a bizarre story, a moment in time when suddenly every NFL fan had an opinion on the science of air pressure.

At the heart of the issue is the fact that every quarterback has his own preference as to the state of the ball. The air pressure can be varied so long as it measures between 12.5 and 13.5 pounds per square inch (psi). This had not been much of a concern in the past: footballs were simply inflated and delivered to the stadium shortly before the start of the game. However, in 2006 the NFL rules were amended to allow balls to be prepared and tested by the quarterback a week prior to the match. These are the balls used while the team is on offence (in possession of the ball); indeed, in the modern game, apart from interceptions, a team will rarely handle one of their opponent's footballs.

During the first half of the crucial AFC Championship playoff match – the winner going through to the Super Bowl – Brady had a throw intercepted by Colts linebacker D'Qwell Jackson, who threw the ball to his equipment manager for safekeeping as a souvenir. Having inspected the ball, at half-time Colts management notified NFL officials about a potential problem. When the Patriots' footballs were measured, 11 were found to be below the legal minimum, one by almost 2 psi. Each one was reinflated to meet the correct specifications and the match continued, New England winning by a huge margin of 45–7.

IS UNDERINFLATION AN ADVANTAGE?

So would there have been any advantage in slightly deflating the football? In the first place, removing air makes the ball softer and so easier to hold, throw and catch. The match also took place in the rain, which normally makes it harder to handle the ball – this is the reason why quarterbacks often wear gloves in cold and wet conditions. But a softer ball would again be easier to grip, even if it was wet. So was the Patriots' heavy win down to the low air pressure in the balls? It's doubtful. They'd only led 17–7 at the end of the first half and once the balls had been reinflated they added a further 28 points.

NFL INQUIRY

Unsurprisingly, the NFL announced an immediate inquiry, but the Patriots' head coach Bill Belichick claimed to have no knowledge of the matter, saying that like every other quarterback Tom Brady had his own personal ball preferences. Brady himself branded the allegations as 'ridiculous'. Scenting a possible scandal, media interest quickly began to shift from the sports pages to the TV news networks and on 23 January the NFL hired attorney Ted Wells to look into what was now being called 'Deflategate'.

Wells's investigation took four months to prepare and it relied heavily on scientific data provided by physicist Dr Daniel Marlow from Princeton. Marlow determined that the balls could not have lost that much air through normal game use, leakage or even 'vigorous rubbing'. He also took into account the temperature impact on the air pressure: a ball inflated in a warm environment will lose pressure when the temperature falls. His report reached a rather ambivalent conclusion: he suggested that it was 'more than probable' that the Patriots had attempted to circumvent the rules of the sport and that Tom Brady had been aware of the deflated balls. Announcing its sanctions the NFL was critical of Brady, claiming that he had failed to cooperate with the investigators. As a result, he was to be suspended without pay for four games. The Patriots were also handed a $1 million (£770,000) fine and lost two picks in the following season's draft.

Buffalo fans hold a sign teasing Tom Brady of the New England Patriots, but they went on to beat Buffalo 41–25.

SOURCE OF DEBATE

The report was controversial and heavily debated in the sports media. Some suggested that coach Belichick should also have been sanctioned and the Patriots disqualified from the Super Bowl; CNN, meanwhile, described it as a 'phoney scandal'. Deflategate had already been the subject of mockery on *Saturday Night Live* and had also found itself parodied in an episode of a popular animated sitcom, *South Park*.

In the aftermath of the scandal, Tom Brady made a successful appeal to have his suspension overturned in

... the balls could not have lost that much air through normal game use.

the United States District Court for the Southern District of New York. However, this judgment was reversed by the Appeals Court in April 2016. When Brady's petitioning of the Court of Appeals was denied he finally agreed to accept his punishment.

The only real legacy of Deflategate is that the NFL changed its inspection rules so that designated match officials would formally check the condition of each football and record its psi measurement.

As far as Tom Brady and the Patriots were concerned, it would be little more than a minor inconvenience. On 1 February 2015 New England beat the Seattle Seahawks 28–24 to win Super Bowl XLIX. Tom Brady was named as the game's Most Valuable Player (MVP) with a record-breaking performance of 37 completed passes from 62 attempts, 328 passing yards, four touchdowns and two interceptions – a record he himself would break two years later at Super Bowl LI. On 3 February 2019, at the age of 41, Brady took a record-breaking sixth Super Bowl title with the Patriots. Whatever the rights and wrongs of Deflategate, few would disagree that he is now the greatest quarterback in NFL history.

New England Patriots quarterback Tom Brady deflects questions about Deflategate with a wry expression on his face.

SKEWING THE ODDS

In the second century AD, the writer Pausanias gives us the earliest documented case of cheating in sport, when the pentathlete Callippius of Athens was fined after trying to bribe his opponents. A more brazen example comes from the Roman historian Suetonius who described how in AD 67 the emperor Nero bribed organizers to postpone the Olympic Games so he could take part in the ten-horse chariot race himself. Despite being thrown from his cart, he was crowned winner.

BASEBALL WORLD SERIES THROWN

In the modern era, the first team sport to have been persistently plagued by match fixing was baseball. The first recorded incident took place at a match in 1865 between the New York Mutuals and Eckford, when Mutuals catcher Bill Wansley was approached by a local gambler to throw the game for $100 (£77). He played so poorly that rumours circulated immediately. Favourites New York were beaten. After an inquiry, Wansley admitted to taking the bribe and was banned from baseball; the Mutuals were also temporarily expelled.

Baseball became a professional sport in 1869, but the betting and match fixing scandals would persist. In 1919 came the mother of all team sports scandals. The World Series saw the Cincinnati Reds pitted against the hot favourites, the Chicago White Sox, the 1917 winners. The White Sox players were notoriously underpaid, and the sport's 'reserve clause' prevented players who refused a new contract from joining another team without permission. By all accounts, the White Sox locker room was not a harmonious place.

Weeks before the World Series was due to begin, White Sox first baseman Chick Gandil was approached by professional gambler Joseph J. Sullivan, who offered him $35,000 (£27,000) – almost nine times his contract salary – to assemble a syndicate of players to throw the Series. Seven other White Sox players came in on the deal, to earn $10,000 (£7,800) each. The money, it was said, was provided by notorious New York organized crime boss Arnold Rothstein. At first the White Sox had been the heavy favourites, but in the days

Star 'hurlers' of the White Sox back in the day: left, Claude 'Lefty' Williams, and, right, Eddie Cicotte.

running up to the first game the odds quickly shifted as large amounts of cash were placed on Cincinnati. During the first game White Sox pitcher Eddie Cicotte, one of the best in the game, made a series of uncharacteristic blunders and the Reds were victorious by an astonishing 9 to 1. Cincinnati ended up taking their first-ever World Series by five games to three.

Although suspicions of foul play were rife, few within the sport had an appetite for such a major scandal. The press had no such reservations, though, with journalist Hugh Fullerton famously running an article titled: 'Is Big League Baseball Being Run for Gamblers, With Players in on the Deal?' In spite of the rumours nothing happened until a year later, when one of the gamblers involved, Bill Maharg, decided to go public.

Eddie Cicotte was the first of the players to crack, giving a tearful testimony to the grand jury: 'I don't know why I did it ... I needed the money. I had the wife and kids.' He was followed by star hitter 'Shoeless' Joe Jackson. In October 1920 eight of Chicago's players – now being dubbed the 'Black Sox' – were indicted on nine counts of conspiracy. However, as their trial began in June 1921, it was discovered that every one of their grand jury confessions had mysteriously disappeared, so the eight players were all acquitted. Arnold Rothstein was suspected of being behind the vanishing evidence, but he never faced prosecution.

The players may have been cleared by the court, but baseball's first commissioner, federal judge Kenesaw Mountain Landis, took his own stand, decreeing that an example had to be set: 'No player who throws a ball game, no player who undertakes or promises to throw a ball game ... will ever play professional baseball again.' The eight disgraced players were then banned from professional baseball for life.

MATCH FIXING IN AMERICAN FOOTBALL

In 1906 there came the first match fixing scandal in American professional football. The Canton Bulldogs and the Massillon Tigers were Ohio rivals and two of the country's top clubs, but Canton's coach, Blondy Wallace, was a shady character with suspected underworld connections. When the Bulldogs were beaten 13–6 in a game they were strong favourites to win, it was alleged that Wallace had paid players to throw the game. After this was printed in the local press the scandal destroyed public faith in professional football and crowd numbers plummeted. It was reckoned that the collapse of the sport in Ohio paved the way for football to blossom in other parts of the country.

In 1946 newspapers would report on efforts to fix the outcome of the NFL Championship between the New York Giants and the Chicago Bears. A professional gambler named Alvin J. Paris offered Giants stars Frank Filchock and Merle Hapes $2,500 (£1,920) each to throw the game, along with the winnings of two $1,000 (£780) bets placed on their behalf. However, suspicious movement on the betting odds the week before the game alerted the police and wiretaps placed on Paris's phone recorded mentions of the two players. When investigated, both admitted that a bribe attempt had been made but they claimed they had declined the money. Their statements were called into question when, against all expectations, Chicago won the game 24–14. Filchock and Hapes always claimed innocence and went unpunished, but Paris was shown to have made a career out of bribing star athletes, allegedly including world champion boxer Rocky Marciano. He was sentenced to a year in prison.

ITALIAN SOCCER SCANDAL

Surprisingly, as the world's biggest sport, soccer has remained relatively unsullied by match-fixing. Far and away the biggest scandal took place in 2006 when Italian police intercepted phone calls between top officials that suggested evidence of suspicious behaviour. The main culprits were Luciano Moggi, general manager of Serie A champions Juventus, and Pierluigi Pairetto, the man responsible for the allocation of referees in Italian club matches. Leading teams were attempting to influence the outcome of matches by having 'favourable' referees selected. The repercussions for the clubs involved were severe: Juventus were stripped of their 2004–5 title and relegated to Serie B; Milan began the next campaign with a 30-point deficit; and other clubs were banned from European competitions for a year. Dubbed 'Calciopoli', the scandal rocked Italian soccer, and resulted in many of the league's top players moving to clubs in Britain and Spain.

THE ETERNAL TEMPTATION

As we've seem time and time again, whenever a sport is rocked by a match-fixing scandal the immediate reaction is primarily concerned with limiting public relations damage, with new 'measures' hastily cobbled together and assurances that no repetition could happen again. Yet with the global sports betting market now estimated to be worth upwards of $250 billion (£192bn) – and growing – the temptation to use illegal means to influence the outcome of a sporting event is surely now greater than ever.

From left to right: Juventus general manager Luciano Moggi, former prime minister of Italy and owner of AC Milan Silvio Berlusconi and AC Milan deputy president Adriano Galliani in 2006. Moggi said that he regretted ever meeting Berlusconi and Galliani, who he claimed were responsible for dragging the reputation of Italian football through the mud.